D1349479

CHANGING ATTITUDES OF BLACK SOUTH AFRICANS TOWARD THE UNITED STATES

David Hirschmann

African Studies
Volume 12

The Edwin Mellen Press
Lewiston/Queenston/Lampeter

Library of Congress Cataloging-in-Publication Data

Hirschmann, David.
Changing attitudes of Black South Africans toward the United States / by David Hirschmann.
p. cm. -- (African studies ; vol. 12)
Bibliography: p.
Includes index.
ISBN 0-88946-192-9
1. United States--Relations--South Africa. 2. South Africa--Relations--United States. 3. Blacks--South Africa--Attitudes. 4. United States--Foreign public opinion, South African. 5. Public opinion--South Africa. I. Title. II. Series: African studies (Lewiston, N.Y.) ; v. 12
E183.8.S6H57 1989
303.4' 8273068--dc20 89-9420
CIP

This is volume 12 in the continuing series
African Studies
Volume 12 ISBN 0-88946-192-9
AS Series ISBN 0-88946-175-9

A CIP catalog record for this book
is available from the British Library.

The Edwin Mellen Press
Box 450
Lewiston, NY
USA 14092

The Edwin Mellen Press
Box 67
Queenston, Ontario
CANADA L0S 1L0

The Edwin Mellen Press, Ltd.
Lampeter, Dyfed, Wales,
UNITED KINGDOM SA48 7DY

Printed in the United States of America

TABLE OF CONTENTS

ACKNOWLEDGMENTS

I wish to express my very sincere gratitude to Peter Vale and Bill Davies of the Institute of Social and Economic Research at Rhodes University in South Africa who saw the point of this research project from the outset and gave encouragement and assistance throughout.

I want to thank Rhodes University for providing me with a Fellowship and practical support to undertake the Research; the Overseas Development Council in Washington D.C. for providing assistance with travel for the first round of interviews; the Ford Foundation for providing a travel grant for the second round of interviews; and the office staff and management of the Institute of Social and Economic Research at Rhodes University, and Ann Held of the International Development Program at The American University, for assistance with, and advice on, the word processing and production of this study.

Many people in South Africa, both Black and White, assisted this project by way of advice - and a great deal was needed - and introductions to interviewees. Ninety-three Black South Africans agreed to be interviewed, some of them twice. I am deeply indebted to all of them for the time they spent with me and the trust they demonstrated during extremely difficult times. I have tried to report their divergent views accurately. Given the circumstances prevailing in South Africa it would seem inappropriate to name any of these people without whose cooperation this project obviously would have been impossible. For what it may be worth this Study is dedicated to them.

David Hirschmann
Washington D.C.
July 1989

THIRD WORLD REVOLUTIONS AND THE UNITED STATES: THE SOUTH AFRICAN CASE

a) A RELEVANT MODEL? THIRD WORLD REVOLUTIONS AND THE UNITED STATES

With the exception of anti-colonial struggles, most examples of serious and sustained civil disorder relate, in the first instance, to domestic, and not foreign, relations. Yet as the conflict continues and grows in intensity (say from demonstrations and strikes to sabotage and on to urban and/or guerilla warfare), the leadership, and then the followers (after some time, and possibly with less intensity) of the evolving revolutionary movement, come to see significant, even vital, connections between foreign powers and the national ruling class which oppresses them. Partly, this broader perception of their conflict occurs because those connections are in reality very important to the capacity of the state to retain effective control. But partly, it may be a result of a changed framework of analysis of the leadership, and a consequent altered socialization of the rank and file.

When the uprising is against a pro-Western, capitalist state, the United States, as the dominant Western capitalist power, is inevitably seen by at least some of the oppressed as supportive of the local ruling class. As the resistance continues, practical support in terms of arms and training and uninhibited diplomatic support come from Eastern countries. By contrast, Western powers, notably the USA, do not assist the revolution; they may provide sporadic and inconsistent diplomatic support, but in practical terms they will hamper the struggle. As the conflict continues, the perception of the United States as a close ally of the oppressor government strengthens: witness the "anti-United States imperialism" language of the Sandinistas, and the regular use of the phrase "the United States-Marcos dictatorship" in the pre-Aquino Philippines. The United States may eventually have to watch its "ally" be overthrown. Or, at some stage, it may intervene and participate in facilitating the transfer of power (as with Somoza in Nicaragua, and Marcos in the Philippines) hoping by so doing to lay the basis for some understanding with the new leadership.

Implied in this suggested model is a continuum of assumed linkages. First, it is assumed that the longer the revolution continues the more radical the revolutionary movement will become. Radicalism, it is also assumed, will mean that in the domestic domain the movement will increasingly see its fight as essentially relating to control over the means of production and to class conflict. An enhanced emphasis upon the dynamics of class and capitalism will in turn lead to a greater appreciation of international political and economic connections, and therefore to a realization that the struggle is against imperialism as well. This type of radicalism will ensure that the mutual antagonism between the movement on the one hand, and domestic and international capital on the other, will intensify. It is next anticipated that this alienation from the West (usually aggravated by the early unresponsiveness of the West to the material and military needs of the movement) will result in the leaders of the insurgents turning to the East for assistance;

which they will receive. At this stage an assessment by the movement of its international friends and enemies will reinforce the leaders' determination to structure a socialist society after the revolution. And domestic socialism implies, if not a pro-Eastern foreign policy, at least a policy of assertive non-alignment with a probable pro-Eastern tinge to it. With some minor variations this has been the case in all three of southern Africa's recent wars of liberation, namely Angola, Mozambique and Zimbabwe.

A primary purpose of this Study is to find out to what extent this is occurring amongst Black South Africans, and in particular what is happening to their attitudes toward the United States.

b) THE SOUTH AFRICAN CASE

There is a tendency to term a major civil uprising a "revolution" only after it has succeeded or come close to a success. While the final outcome of the past twelve or so years of strife in South Africa remains uncertain - at the time of writing it had suffered a setback - its dimensions amounted to something akin to a revolution in terms of breadth and depth of hostility, the determination to demonstrate and express that hostility, the period of sustained violence and disruption, the suffering involved and the acceptance of that suffering as essential to change, and the uncompromising and increasingly fundamental objectives of the movement.

The conflict had, of course, been there for centuries. The movement for change had been building up for most of this century. It had never been allowed to gain effective momentum. The situation which existed from roughly 1976 to 1986 was different: it represented a broad, serious and sustained threat to the continuation of White rule. Tom Lodge, in the last chapter of his work on Black politics, wrote:

> The resistance of the 1970s provides a startling contrast in terms of scale and duration to the movements of the 1950s and early 1960s. This has reflected a fundamental crisis in South African society, in its origins both economic and political, a crisis which the authorities are apparently incapable of resolving through reform. The particular drama central to this book has seen its cast swollen by hundreds of thousands, and the intimate localised scenarios through which we have viewed earlier acts are no longer appropriate. Resistance itself has become one of the components of this crisis.[1]

Early in the 1960s the South African Government had managed to quell Black resistance through the use of force, imprisonments, legislative restrictions and an effective police information network. Black leaders were imprisoned or banned or fled the country, and the two principal Black political movements, the African National Congress (ANC) and the Pan-Africanist Congress (PAC) were proscribed. That section of the leadership which had escaped detention went into exile and took the remnants of their organizations with them. Based on this restoration of law and order, business confidence returned and by the mid-60s the economy was booming. Black opposition was rendered temporarily comatose. There was tranquility for Whites and their privilege appeared once again secure.

A decade later this system was to confront the commencement of its most serious and sustained challenge. Primarily for readers who are unfamiliar with recent events in South Africa, this section of the chapter will trace very briefly the steps leading up to, and the events which made up, this period of the Black struggle. In doing so it will introduce - also very briefly - the main Black organizations and tendencies, an understanding of which is essential to the Study which follows.

A large measure of credit for the resuscitation of Black opposition must go to the Black Consciousness (BC) movement. This political and ideological tendency found its origins at the Blacks-only universities established by the ruling National Party in fulfillment of its ideal of separate education at all levels. Students like those at the University of the North (at Turfloop in the Northern Transvaal) for example were stuck out in isolated bush campuses where they were taught and administered mainly by Afrikaners sympathetic to apartheid. In a very real sense the BC movement was therefore the stepchild of apartheid. In 1969 some Black students broke away from the mostly white liberal National Union of South African Students to form their own Blacks-only South African Students Organization (SASO). Its inaugural conference was held at the University of the North in July 1969.

> Black Consciousness stressed the unity of all blacks including Coloureds and Indians, and the need for them to separate themselves from White liberals in order to develop their own 'militant self reliance,' overcome their feelings of racial inferiority, and rediscover the achievements of African history and culture and the 'communalism' of 'traditional' African society. [It] particularly attracted young black students, high school pupils, professionals and clergymen in the towns and cities ... during the 1976 unrest, it proved to be the decisive mobilizing ideology for united black action on the university and school campus.[2]

Whether it was "the decisive" (as Lewis, and Kane-Berman[3] suggest) or "a decisive" mobilizing force is a matter of some controversy. Lodge, in taking note of different perspectives on this, asserts that as far as young urban middle class Africans were concerned it was the dominant intellectual influence in their political perceptions, and further that in a "distilled" form it "percolated down to a much broader and socially amorphous group."[4]

If the BC movement developed as a top-down intellectual process the reemergence of Black trade unions took place as a spontaneous bottom-up movement, a practical manifestation of worker frustration as small increases to their already very low wages failed to respond to accelerating inflation. In the first few months of 1973, Black workers at factories in Natal came out in a series of unorganized strikes which ended South Africa's labor peace and rudely reinserted the reality of Black labor power into an understanding of both the economy and the politics of the country. In the first three months of that year, 160 strikes involving 61,000 workers took place.[5] The State had the legal authority and the capacity to imprison the workers and react against them with violent means. Between the Government and business a decision was made not to do so. Ad hoc negotiations took place and wages were raised. Even if this amounted to a less than fully conscious analysis of the situation, it indicated an acknowledgement by the White political and economic leadership of the importance both quantitatively (in terms of numbers) and qualitatively (in terms of skills) of Black labor. Black labor realized that this had been realized. Strikes spread. Embryonic worker organizations proliferated.

In earlier periods "a central problem in the development of black trade unions in South Africa [had] been the rupturing of the process of maturation by the failure to win management recognition as well as by state hostility.... Before the 1970s there had been three major thrusts toward African unionization in South Africa's labour history - in the 1920s; during World War II; and in the 1950s and early 1960s. Each wave of unionization [had been] followed by repressive legislation."[6] According to Eddie Webster:

> In the wake of the crushing of worker organizations in the early 1960s, the South African economy grew as never before. By 1976 an exceptionally high degree of concentration of economic power - a system of monopoly capital - existed.... The process which saw the consolidation of monopoly capital in South Africa also led to a correspond-

> ing growth of the black working class, bringing black workers firmly to the centre of the stage. In particular it led to the growth of the semi-skilled black worker - the organizational base for the industrial unions.[7]

This time the process of maturation has not been ruptured. At first, de facto, by the end of the decade, de jure, Black trade unions were recognized. Business has tested them and Government has harassed them; but they have steadily strengthened and consolidated their positions and broadened their foci of concern from the factory to the community to the national level. The Council of South African Trade Unions (Cosatu) has emerged in recent years as the main federation of trade unions, growing rapidly in numbers, consolidating a disparate group of unions, and creatively containing the tensions between those who wish to stress political issues and those who wish to attend to specifically worker concerns. In the process it has suffered large scale arrests of its leadership, and its headquarters have been bombed. As a headline in the South African *Weekly Mail* read: "Bombed. Banned. Shot at. Abducted. Murdered. Still kicking. Despite a year of adversity Cosatu congress this week is unlikely to adapt a meeker line."[8] While ideologically and operatively it is close to the ANC and accepts the Freedom Charter (see below), it stresses the need to remain autonomous from political organizations and for working class leadership in the struggle for liberation. A smaller but nonetheless significant federation of unions is the National Council of Trade Unions (Nactu). It too stresses the need for autonomy and worker leadership, but ideologically it is closer to the evolving notions of Black Consciousness.

The spread of Black Consciousness and the recommencement of worker assertiveness were followed by the collapse in 1974 of Portuguese colonialism in the neighboring states of Mozambique and Angola, and the coming to power the following year of Frelimo in the former and the Movimento Popular de Libertacao de Angola (MPLA) in the latter. This altered the power equation in the southern African region; White rule in Rhodesia now looked very shaky, Namibia was more vulnerable, and South Africa - its protective Portuguese buffer having suddenly disappeared - found itself confronted directly by two hostile radically-oriented states. The victories of Frelimo and MPLA also gave a boost to Black morale in South Africa, particularly among the youth.

The following year the Black youth initiated their own uprising. In 1976 the Government announced that arithmetic and social studies would be taught in the Afrikaans language at Black schools. Black high school pupils - their level of political awareness having been raised by the BC movement - had long been angered at the inferior education they received. They were also becoming increasingly despondent about their future economic prospects. This announcement acted as a catalyst transforming that anger and despondency into a youth movement that shocked the system into a series of cruel responses which in turn raised the level of commitment and hostility of the youth yet further. On June 16, in Soweto, a large Black city outside of Johannesburg, the Police killed two and injured other demonstrating pupils. Rioting followed and it spread quickly to other parts of the country. The youth went beyond these early outbursts of anger to create and support new organizations and play a leading role in organizing boycotts stay-aways and demonstrations.

Lodge and Swilling distinguish between two types of youth organization, both of which proliferated in the urban areas of the country. The first were known in the Eastern Cape as Amabuthu (the Xhosa word for the warriors who resisted the settler invasion in the nineteenth century) but also as young lions, comrades, the guerillas, and the soldiers. They were typically boys between 12 and 16 with at most a few years schooling, unemployed, virtually illiterate, the offspring of broken or scattered families, "living in packs one hundred or two hundred strong in what they called 'bases' on the fringes of the poorer squatter camps." The second was the school movement which formed organizations such as the Congress of South African Students (Cosas) and demonstrated a sophisticated understanding of the Freedom Charter.

> Their advocacy of socialism may be informed by a concept of class struggle, as well as by an awareness of the outside world. Their iconography will include not only Nelson Mandela, Walter Sisulu and Govan Mbeki, but also Julius Nyerere, Samora Machel, Karl Marx, and even Vladimir Lenin. Unlike the Amabuthu, they will be consciously non-racist; for them the enemy is the 'bourgeoisie' not just 'the Boer,' and the student leaders will often have had a degree of contact with white 'progressive' groups and individuals.[9]

A study of a series of consumer boycotts in one small town, Grahamstown, illustrated the central role of the youth in organizing and educating their communities.[10] The continuing ability of the youth to disturb and disrupt, and the Government's inability to find any constructive response added indirectly to the country's growing economic woes. Somehow in the eyes of foreigners South Africa was no longer as secure an investment risk as it used to be.

Following the example of their children, Blacks throughout the country began to establish grassroots organizations of all kinds, including street committees, area committees and civic associations. It was as if there was a sudden realization that participatory organizations give power, strengthen confidence, and enhance community control, and that one can go ahead and establish them without waiting for Government initiative or clearance.

> In bare outline the structure of this street/area committee system is as follows. The residents of a particular street attend a regular meeting at which various issues ... are discussed. They then elect one representative who, together with the representatives of other street committees, form an area committee (normally an area covers about 16 or 20 streets). The area committee then links up with the leadership of the civic and youth organizations ... at the highest level.[11]

In embryo, as one of the people interviewed stated, these organizations provided an alternative structure to that offered by the Government. It also provided a warning to Pretoria that "peoples' power" might go beyond the rhetorical stage and become institutionalized.

The principal beneficiary of these developments was South Africa's oldest and most widely accepted Black political organization, the African National Congress (ANC). Despite its long period in exile, its support from Black South Africans had not dissipated. Even at its least effective moments its principal message, the presence of its leaders, notably Nelson Mandela, in South African prisons, and Pretoria's continual denigrating of the organization (with frequent reference to it being a "communist" and "terrorist" organization) kept it alive in the minds of the people. In addition, it had managed to win considerable international recognition for its cause. Despite the frustrations, the divisions and the setbacks of those years, the ANC had by the mid-seventies regained the organizational capacity to take advantage of the new strategic possibilities offered by the Frelimo Government in Mozambique, absorb the large numbers of new young recruits who fled the Government's attempts to smash the youth movement, and reinfiltrate its members back into South Africa for purposes of sabotage, education and organization. Although it remains an illegal organization, it is widely and openly acknowledged by most politically aware Blacks to be the organization in which they place their hopes for bringing about change; and acceptance by the ANC has become the touchstone of legitimacy of legal organizations.

In the US much attention is given to the long standing alliance between the ANC and the South African Communist Party. While this Party undoubtedly has more influence at the decision-making level than might seem appropriate given its small membership, its influence has been exaggerated; a point carefully and convincingly made by Tom Karis recently in *Foreign Affairs*.[12] Further, this is balanced by a wide variety of ideological tendencies included in the organization. Merle Lipton observed - and this is a broadly accepted assessment- that the ANC encompasses a broad range of views: social democrats who favor a mixed economy and non-racialism; Marxists who agree with the non-racialism, but want nationalization of the means of production; and Africanists, who might be capitalist or socialist, but whose prime objective is African rule.[13] Uhlig makes a similar point about its membership and support being diverse, and sees its commonality in the consistent support for "its original populist manifesto - the Freedom Charter," accepted in 1955, and calling for universal suffrage, racial equality, freedom of association and of religion, and a sharing of the country's wealth and land. In his view, it "could hardly be construed as revolutionary by Western democratic standards. Although it contains mild references to land reform and to redistribution of mineral and other national wealth, those provisions too, could hardly be found surprising."[14] The essential non-racialism of the Charter and of its adherents, and of the ANC and its followers, has returned to challenge some of the original notions of Black Consciousness and, according to Gavin Lewis, has reasserted its dominance in Black politics.[15] This topic is taken up by the interviewees in some detail in Chapter 4.

All this widespread divergent activity appeared in need of some overarching coordination at the national level. The impetus toward the formation of organizations to perform such a role was provided by the decision of the South African Government to initiate a tricameral parliamentary system. One house would be for Whites, one for Coloreds, and one for Indians. The arrangements ensured that Whites could not be defeated on any issue of significance; but of more importance they excluded Africans. While the Government held these proposals out as reforms which for the first time allowed people of color to participate in decision-making at the national level, most Black leaders rejected it "as an attempt by the government to modernise and entrench, rather than abolish, apartheid."

> Out of anger and rejection there grew in 1983 two new mass-based black unity alliances - the United Democratic Front (UDF) and the National Forum (NF). Although both organisations were loose coalitions of broadly like-minded interest groups rather than tightly knit and ideologically uniform political bodies, they did tend to develop distinctive and different public policy stands. The UDF, although it also contains a broad range of ideological viewpoints, tends for its part to follow Charterist lines, and stresses non-racialism, actively recruiting white support. It also emphasises the 'primacy of the working class in the national democratic struggle', but displays a greater ambiguity on the issue of the desirability of a socialist alternative. ... The UDF consists of a range of affiliated civic and community organisations, as well as some trade unions and sporting, religious and professional bodies. Committed to a policy of non-collaboration with the new constitutional structures, the UDF aims at a 'free, democratic and non-racial South Africa.' By December 1983 it claimed over 500 affiliates with a combined membership of 1,5 million.[16]

Its inclusion of a wide range of ideological viewpoints, its non-racialism, the political sympathies of its leadership, its pragmatism which includes nevertheless an emphasis on the role of workers, and its adherence to the Charter make it a natural legal partner to the ANC.

The NF, the smaller of the two organizations in terms of membership, is primarily an alliance of the Black Consciousness Movement organizations led by the Azanian People's Organization (Azapo) and the Western Cape-based Unity Movement with a long-standing intellectual commitment to an analysis and a strategy based on the centrality of class rather than race. In light of the original rationale for the BC movement, this might appear a strange partnership; but given the directions in which it has been evolving their ideological approaches were no longer incompatible. The NF therefore tends to adhere to the present notions of Black Consciousness and excludes Whites from positions of leadership.

> The Forum also stresses a perception of apartheid and capitalism as inextricably intertwined and interdependent. Opposed to ethnic divisions among Blacks, and suspicious of the collaborative tendencies of the black middle classes, the NF advocates an uncompromising rejection not only of the new constitution, but also of capitalism and apartheid as a whole. It proposes instead the 'establishment of a democratic, anti-racist worker Republic in Azania.'[17]

While the ANC has been in a position to take advantage of recent political developments in Black politics, the Pan-Africanist Congress (PAC) has not. Its standing seems to have declined. Representing the "Africanist tendency" - which put more emphasis on race and nationality than the ANC seemed ready to do, and which demanded Black leadership - it broke away in the late fifties.[18] Like the ANC it had to go into exile where it suffered serious and divisive personality and organizational difficulties. Close as it therefore appears ideologically to the BC movement, it does not seem to have forged any working alliances with BC organizations. From the results of polls, and in these interviews, it appears to be weak at the moment. In a total of 110 interviews only two people mentioned the organization.

One other movement is relevant to this Study, namely the Natal-based Inkatha. "Originally founded as a Zulu cultural organisation by the royal house in 1928, Inkatha ... was revived by Chief Gatsha Buthelezi in the early 1970s, and ... in 1975 it began to structure itself as a mass organisation." Its leader, Chief Buthelezi, a grandson of King Dinizulu, the last king of an independent Zulu state, was installed as a chief in 1957 with the apparent approval of Natal ANC leaders. "In 1970 a Kwa Zulu Territorial Authority was established with Chief Buthelezi as its chief executive officer. Two years later Buthelezi was appointed as chief executive councillor of the Kwa Zulu Legislative Assembly."[19] Chief Buthelezi has consistently criticized apartheid, arguing that he has utilized the system in order to bring change, and he has refused to accept Government offers of independence for the Zulu bantustan. His "Inkatha movement has become almost inseparable from state structures in Kwa Zulu, with its influence on school syllabuses, its community development projects, and the interlocking of political and administrative office."[20] Buthelezi is in favor of foreign investment, the West, and capitalism. In his words, "Inkatha sees that Western influences which come about with imported capitalism, management and technology have an uplifting effect and promote Black advancement";[21] and again, "The free enterprise system goes hand in hand with democratic government and ... social order based on western industrialised values." He attacks socialism and one-party ideas which he claims the ANC Mission in exile wants for South Africa.[22]

This brief sketch has touched no more than the surface of a complicated and dynamic situation. For purposes of facilitating understanding of the Report which follows, the position will be simplified yet further. Three principal political tendencies will be referred to throughout the Study. Each tendency will include, with the principal political organizations, the ideologically proximate trade union and youth organizations. First, the ANC/UDF/Charterist tendency which is assumed to be by far the largest and ideologically most disparate of the three. Although it retains a certain distance from the ANC and the UDF, Cosatu is included here because of its ideological closeness and cooperative methods of operation. Second, is the Black Consciousness/National Forum/Azapo grouping. In 1987 the two trade union federations closest to it, namely Cusa and Azactu, merged to form the National Council of Trade Unions (Nactu), and this will be seen as part of this tendency. The third is Chief Buthelezi's Inkatha, the support for which is to be found mainly in parts of Natal and among some Zulu people. The United Workers' Union of South Africa (Uwusa) is the affiliated trade union.

c) THE MODEL AND THE SOUTH AFRICAN CASE

In accordance with the simple model set out in the first part of this chapter, the White rulers in South Africa are pro-Western (President Botha has made much of this), capitalist (and of this too) and have long received effective backing from domestic and international corporations, and, despite the critical rhetoric, from major Western governments, such as the UK, the US, West Germany, and Japan as well. Capitalism- and this would be acknowledged even by many of those favoring its continuation in the country - has long exploited very cheap Black South African labor, in the main utilizing the controls of apartheid for this purpose. Leading Black businessmen who are strong supporters of a free enterprise system acknowledged at a conference held in 1987 that the source of Black antagonism to capitalism derived from the inequities that the system had generated.[23] They also pondered the dilemmas of their own position. As a keynote speaker pointed out, "the

Black middle class was a prime example of a state created middle class ... it could not have come about except at the pleasure of the ruling establishment for purposes inimical to the black nationalist cause ... the middle class were to be given a stake in the status quo so as to be a buffer against the 'radical masses.'"[24]

In response to this protracted period of abuse, angry, assertive and well-organized Black trade unions have developed. They have stressed their independence from the main political movements along the following lines:

> All the great [liberation] movements have not been able to deal with the particular and fundamental problem of the workers. It is, therefore, essential that workers must strive to build their own powerful and effective organisation even whilst they are part of the wider popular struggle ... to ensure that the popular movement is not hijacked by elements who will in the end have no option but to turn against their worker supporters.[25]

Not only have they set out to retain an autonomous position, but they have consistently called for working class and trade union leadership of the struggle. This is explained by Cyril Ramaphosa of the Mineworkers' Union:

> What we mean is that you have to look at the working class and maybe even try to come to a definition of 'working class'. By working class, we mean all those people who do not own the means of production. They may be working, or be unemployed, or be in service organizations, like hospitals, and so forth. As far as we are concerned, they are part and parcel of the working class. Now, the organized workers, should say under the banner of Cosatu ... take up the leadership positions in a concerted struggle to gain liberation in our country.... We believe that the workers should take leadership positions because we would like to see a country that is going to be ruled in the interests of the workers who produce the wealth of the country.[26]

Prominent UDF officials have acknowledged the significance of the working class in the movement. For example, Murphy Morobe, publicity secretary of the UDF, has argued that this leadership of the democratic movement was not understood as purely trade union leadership but as "mass working class leadership of the UDF itself."[27]

It is important, therefore, to note the growing anti-capitalist sentiment espoused by the major unions. Jay Naidoo, General Secretary of Cosatu, told a meeting at the University of Natal:

> It is our experience that apartheid racism has gone hand in hand with our exploitation and suffering at the hands of the bosses. Free enterprise has not been something separate and hostile to racism.... the root and fruit of the apartheid tree is the exploitation of workers in South Africa. ... To us the alliance between big business and the apartheid state is soaked in the blood of workers.[28]

Cosatu resolutions on multinational corporations also reveal a fundamentally negative analysis of their operation, and an intention to educate workers to understand that economic exploitation, super profits and starvation wages are an integral part of the "brutal system of national oppression and capitalist exploitation."[29] Elijah Barayi, first President of Cosatu, affirmed that his organization would nationalize the mines and was socialist in nature. He wanted to see a socialist South Africa, along the lines of the British Labor Party and based on a multi-party democracy.[30]

It is also important to point out that many of the methods of resistance pit poor Black people against business - consumer boycotts, strikes, stay-aways - and one assumes that the experiential educational impact of these measures must be to demonstrate the role of business in the system of oppression and so strengthen class consciousness. This should not be simplified however. A study of consumer boycotts in Grahamstown concluded that the pervasiveness of inequality along racial lines tended to minimize the salience of class inequality insofar as the people's experience and consciousness were concerned.[31]

Also pursuant to the model, the main liberation movements sought material and military assistance from the principal Western powers, but were rebuffed. They therefore turned to the Eastern Bloc from where they have received consistent military help, as did their allies in Mozambique, Angola, Namibia and Zimbabwe. The ANC's alliance with the South African Communist Party has facilitated the flow of assistance from the Soviet Union and its allies. In addition, the training of their soldiers has been by East German, Cuban and other Eastern Bloc instructors. In addition to military training, other education opportunities have been provided. For example, according to Uhlig, the movement was invited to place more than 300 students a year in Soviet-bloc universities, and returning students have had an important intellectual influence among their peers. At a diplomatic level, ANC officials receive far greater formal respect in the Eastern Bloc than in the West; and of the Western governments, the US has remained by far the most estranged from the ANC.[32] Encouraging this process has been their cooperative alliances with the major liberation movements in Mozambique, Angola and Zimbabwe. In all three cases, prolonged struggles appeared to transform nationalist movements into socialist ones, and after victory these emerged as radical Marxist or socialist Governments.

Other possible influences include the diplomatic need to retain mutually supportive links with other liberation movements. While there is no ideological uniformity among these groups it is of interest to note that in official ANC messages Oliver Tambo greets "the PLO, the Palestinian people, the Saharoui Arab Democratic Republic, the Farabundi Marti of El Salvador, Fretilin of East Timor, as well as the embattled people of Nicaragua and the progressive forces organized in the Sandinista National Liberation Front."[33] The rhetoric of the ANC does sometimes take on strong anti-capitalist tones and even if it is only rhetoric it will have an influence on its followers. An example would be Tambo's comments on Western interests made in a speech to a third world conference in 1986: "they support racism because it expresses the imperative of the systems they represent, namely, to dominate, and serves their purposes as an instrument for the extreme exploitation of those who are dominated."[34] The ANC's official newspaper, Sechaba, takes a consistently hostile line towards capitalism, the West and the US.

The movement has also been joined since the 1976 Soweto uprising by younger people who have a more positive interest in socialism than some of the older generation. Many of these new recruits are reported to arrive in the training camps expressing an interest in Marxism. The reason for this was recently suggested in an interview with an anonymous African student leader:

> The Mantanzimas and Sebes [this refers to Homeland leaders] taught us it was not a black and white thing, it was not only whites exploiting and oppressing us. We looked for an explanation and found it in a class analysis of society.[35]

They have strengthened the younger and more radical school of ANC thought, which according to Uhlig, sees in the Freedom Charter a much more comprehensive mandate for change. This view emphasizes the economic consequences of South African racism: it concentrates on the poverty and exploitation of Black workers and interprets the ANC struggle as following the pattern of Marxist class conflict. "The popularity of radical ideology among younger ANC members is partly explained by their training in Soviet bloc nations."[36] Politicized Black youth inside the country have also become positively interested in, and must be seen as a pressure group for, socialism.

In addition, there are long-established, ideological traditions among some Black intellectuals and activists favoring communism and socialism. In addition to the South African Communist Party, one finds strong elements in early "Colored" politics in the Western Cape. For example, the Declaration of National Liberation League in the 1930's "interpreted the country's history in terms of imperialist-capitalist rule - an alliance between British imperialists and white capitalists under which white workers were detached from their black counterparts with theories of racial superiority.... It called for working class unity between whites and blacks and the destruction of imperialism in collaboration with the struggles of colonial peoples worldwide."[37] A successor organization, the Non-European Unity Movement which evolved in the forties, retains this theoretical tradition today. As we have seen, this group has now allied itself with the increasingly socialistically inclined BC movement.

Put simply, the principal elements which may be serving to strengthen anti-capitalism and support for socialism are first, the long standing, continuing and blatantly inequitable consequences of the way in which capitalism operates in South Africa; second, the changing ideologies within the country, notably among union leaders, the youth, BC followers and the left of the UDF; and third, the views of certain groups within the ANC.

Yet, in the view of David Lewis, a Cape Town trade unionist, "socialism is not a very developed concept in the discourse of oppositional politics in South Africa." Some of the points he relies on to explain this include Government censorship and general repression preventing debate on socialism; the legitimacy which the movement seeks particularly in the international arena which obliges it to deemphasize talk of class conflict;

and "the theoretical position of the South African Communist Party, which asserts a rigid division between 'two stages' of the South African struggle - the first and current phase being the struggle for national liberation, the second being the struggle for socialism - which has inadvertently retarded the need for socialist discourse in the 'first stage'." It is also hampered by the efforts of Marxist intellectuals to establish a symbiotic relationship between apartheid and capitalism which has "lent weight to the fiction that to fight apartheid is ineluctably to fight capitalism." This too has reduced the need to give attention to socialism. A socialist position too is seen by some as an ultra-left position which might divide the working class from other oppressed people in the country.[38]

The retardation of debate about class as both an analytical and a strategic concern, and about a socialist alternative for South Africa derives directly from the fact that oppression in South Africa has for so long been seen as a case of racial discrimination initiated mainly by the State to protect White privilege, rather than one of class exploitation in which capital and the State cooperate (much - not all - of the time) to ensure the interests of the beneficiary - White - classes. While intellectuals, both Black and White, have convincingly challenged the simplicity of this type of analysis, race has been elevated to such a level of importance by the Government, and, in natural response, by the oppressed, that notions of class exploitation, and imperialism, as analytically valid as they may be, may have a difficult time taking hold in the minds of non-intellectual (a far narrower category than non-educated) Black South Africans. Merle Lipton concluded:

> In the competition for resources, class conflict often took on ethnic form; the lines of cleavage between groups, and the alliances constructed in the political struggle, were usually along ethnic not class lines. Class interests were not submerged, but nor did ethnic/racial feelings fade in the face of the supposedly homogenizing forces of industri-

> alization and urbanization; rather ... they proved unexpectedly persistent.[39]

Obviously, those with the power have been in a position to create, define, manipulate, legislate and adapt race and ethnicity to their own political and economic ends. In turn, those who wish to confront them have to deal with the dual reality. At the level of analysis, class interest may well be the underlying and motivating force behind the structuring of a racist society. Nevertheless, at the level of strategy - at least short term strategy - it is that long-established, racial definition given by the Government to its policies, and the racially specific way in which those policies have impacted themselves, which provide the most significant and facilitative mobilizing and unifying factor for the oppressed. A major challenge to the opposition leadership is that if it responds to a racial definition of society with a racial analysis it is then allowing itself to operate within terms of the hegemonic ideology of apartheid instead of challenging it with a counter ideology.[40] More significantly, it may lead to a misunderstanding of the causes and sources of the oppression and to inappropriate strategies. The ANC has dealt with this in different ways. The Freedom Charter of 1955, for example, is a firmly non-racial document. Its Morogoro Declaration of 1969 recognized the strategic importance of race, noting that in the present context "the national sense of grievance is the most potent revolutionary force which must be harnessed."[41] Today the non-racial emphasis is again strong.

The dominant response to this dilemma has been the two-stage notion of a possible socialist future referred to above by Lewis. This has been accepted as a strategy by the ANC. According to John Saul:

> ... the ANC ... stands in most immediate and overt harmony with the UDF ... the most important above ground manifestation of the "popular-democratic" current in South Africa. Moreover, the ANC remains most comfortable with a rela-

> tively populist projection of its programmatic intentions; it is reluctant, certainly, to proclaim any very straight-forward socialist vision of the future, a "two-stage" theory of the struggle (national liberation first, then, possibly, socialism) still being the most that many of its spokespersons will offer publicly on the subject.[42]

The two-stage approach has a long-standing acceptance in many circles. The idea of postponing the socialist program is in fact favored by many on the left of the movement. The South African Communist Party accepts it. Recently, Victor Gongarov, a Soviet analyst, also has argued that the problem of liberation should be settled first before the idea of socialism is put on the agenda.[43] Also, at the July 1987 Cosatu conference, the ANC, SACP and Sactu (South African Congress of Trade Unions) all sent similar advice to the participants.[44]

In addition to providing a response to the analytical/ strategic dilemma of race and class, the two-stage proposition postpones potentially divisive ideological debate in an organization which includes a wide range of political views,[45] permits the ANC considerable room for maneuver and changing emphases in the area of international diplomacy, allows for a non-binding and loosely defined populist third world rhetoric, and accords with the essentially pragmatic and inclusive leanings of its leaders, particularly the older, more senior ones. In Uhlig's view, this "older group includes noncommunists such as Mandela, Tambo and many other senior ANC officials representing a more traditional or conservative approach to the fight against apartheid grounded in a strong faith in the rule of law ... and British legal traditions ... and an emphasis on political rights" and admiration for the West. "When we grew up" Tambo told him, "we were fascinated by the history of America.... And we thought that if there was any country that would understand our position, it was the United States."[46]

Furthermore, while the major military support has consistently come from the Eastern Bloc, the sources of assistance have broadened considerably, particularly for humanitarian purposes. The ANC has cultivated especially close ties with the Scandinavian nations, which together provide a majority of the group's outright cash assistance. In addition, it receives funds from the United Nations, the Governments of Austria, Italy and a broad cross section of third world nations, and from non-governmental agencies such as Oxfam, the World Council of Churches, the United Churches of Canada, the British Council of Churches, various Catholic aid agencies, and Scandinavian charities.[47] To retain this - according to Karis- it has engaged in a non-doctrinaire and non-aligned search for aid from every source.[48] The ANC also actively courts the support of all the major Western governments.

Inside South Africa there is a growing and influential Black middle class - businessmen, managers, professionals - many of whom support the ANC's general objectives of liberation, but do not favor socialism. And the more farsighted White capitalists have, for some time, been attempting to bolster their numbers and their dedication to the free enterprise system. Further, through strict official censorship and control of education, most Black South Africans will have been denied access to the material on which to build a satisfactory understanding of socialism and the operation of socialist countries. For most people it remains something of a mystery.

In thinking further about Black South Africans and the radical/socialist/anti-American model suggested, one needs to take note also of certain specifics of the relationship of Black South Africans with the US. For a start, the US is not the ex-colonial power (as in the Philippines) nor the dominant geographically proximate power (as in Latin America). Further, the US experience with the civil rights movement may be seen by Black South Africans as having been effective in liberating Black Americans, and therefore indicative of a political system worthy of respect. The diplomacy of the US under leaders like Kennedy and Carter may have left a residue of positive appreciation of long-run US policy intentions, and a readiness to distinguish Reagan's Constructive Engagement from an entity such as "the US Government" or from "the US" as a totality. In response to the Sullivan Principles on proper business behavior, people may have come to distinguish between more enlightened American companies and the US Government. For many decades, US entertainment and mass media have strengthened bonds of music, humor, fashion, and fun: there is a long-standing mass cultural connection between Black South Africans and the people of the US which may have an influence on evolving attitudes. There is no comparable connection with Eastern countries. Thus, while they may become angry with US foreign policy they may still retain respect for the system, including its all-important economic component. In addition, a relatively large number of prominent Black leaders have been educated or have been on extended visits to America.

It is also possible that the unsatisfactory economic performances of some African states with a declared commitment to socialism may have had a dampening effect on interest in socialism. These would include nearby Mozambique and Angola, although many Black South Africans would attribute a major share of responsibility for their difficulties to the destabilizing undertakings of Pretoria.

As the Introduction has made clear, this theme is a central focus of this Study and will be taken up in the interviews.

d) PRINCIPAL POLITICAL AFFILIATIONS

It is impossible to get an accurate assessment of Black support for the major political tendencies since elections are not allowed. In the past few years, however, a number of surveys of urban Black opinion have been carried out. Three of them, all administered by social scientists of standing, were taken into account in the preparation of this Study: Lawrence Schlemmer's *Black Worker Attitudes. Political Options, Capitalism and Investment in South Africa* (1984), Mark Orkin's *Disinvestment, the Struggle and the Future. What Black South Africans Really Think* (1986), and Fatima Meer's *Political and Economic Choices of Disenfranchised South Africans* (1986). For a number of reasons, their significance for this Study could be indicative only and not conclusive. Firstly, they deal with a variety of subjects going well beyond political affiliation. They use different classifications for political groupings or tendencies, and Orkin uses the names of individual leaders as well as groupings. It is not made clear whether different groups might oppose or cooperate (in the event of an election): for example it is unlikely that the UDF would oppose the ANC. They ask questions in different ways, and do not cover exactly the same geographic areas. The three scholars themselves have different political orientations and their results are - not surprisingly - divergent; and controversial.

Their value for the purposes of this exercise, albeit indicative, was sufficient. Their combined findings provided important contextual information in which to locate the Study, and a general but essential sense of roughly the proportions of interviewees of different political affiliations to approach. In the circumstances in which the interviews were carried out it would have been unrealistic to attempt to administer a study intended to be numerically and scientifically exact. Many of those who should have been interviewed were in prison or in hiding; and the interviews sought to elicit in-depth responses rather than to produce survey data. The objective in selecting and balancing the sample of interviewees was to seek out a representative, reasonably well-balanced cross section of political opinion. Other categories going beyond political opinion were also taken into account; these will be discussed below.

As explained, for purposes of this undertaking, three categories of political tendency were delineated: the ANC/-UDF/Charterist group; the Black Consciousness/ National Forum/Azapo grouping; and Inkatha. The results of the three surveys were interpreted and adapted with these three alignments in mind. The adaptations were based on readings on Black politics and discussions with South Africans; their purpose was to make the three surveys roughly comparative, and to provide a very approximate idea of the relative support for the three tendencies. The findings of Schlemmer's, Meer's and Orkin's surveys, brief explanations of the assumptions behind the adaptations, and the adaptations to each of the surveys are contained in the Appendix. (See Tables 2, 3 and 4.) The sample selected for interview was meant to accord - again approximately - with this pattern of political support.

Table 1 (Derived from Tables 2, 3, 4, and 5 in the Appendix.)

COMPARISON OF THE THREE SURVEYS - AS ADAPTED- AND THE SAMPLE INTERVIEWED IN THIS STUDY

TENDENCY	SCHLEMMER	MEER	ORKIN	SAMPLE*
	%			
ANC/UDF	57.4	69.8	75.9	69.8
BC/NF/Azapo	7.4	18.3	2.6	14.0
Inkatha	23.6	8.2	10.4	9.7
Govt/Councillors	11.8	3.3	10.4	-

* Discussed in more detail in the next section. 4.3%, while vaguely sympathetic, distanced themselves from the ANC; and 3.2% seemed to have mixed affiliation to the ANC/UDF and BC/NF tendencies.

e) THE GROUP INTERVIEWED: "THE SAMPLE"

In total, 110 interviews were carried out, 45 during the months of June to August 1986, and a further 65 during the same months of 1987. Of these, 17 people were interviewed in both years, which means that a total of 93 people participated in the Study. In the tables providing information on the sample the 17 who contributed in both 1986 and 1987 are included in 1986 only.

It may be useful, particularly for those who do not find detailed tables pleasant reading, to sum up the principal features of the sample of 93 interviewees. The point must be emphasized that because of the atmosphere within the country at the time (see below) specific questions were not asked about these matters. Occupation was almost always clear from the start; political orientation generally became clear fairly soon after the interview commenced; educational information was forthcoming in about half the cases and the rest were journalists, priests, teachers) 10%, corporation managers and businessmen 7.5%, academics 7.5%, lawyers 7.5%, and technical assistants/secretaries 3%. 84% were men and 16% women. Interviews were carried out in Johannesburg, Durban, Port Elizabeth, Cape Town, Grahamstown and Uitenhage.

If everything had gone perfectly according to plan, I would have wished to have interviewed another two or three businessmen, two or three Inkatha members and half dozen high school students. Meetings to achieve these ends unfortunately broke down on a number of occasions. In terms of ideological balance, the likely relative conservatism of the first two groups would have been counteracted by the probable greater radicalism of the youth. Overall, it was an urban-based, educated, politically aware group, representative of the major Black political tendencies opposed to apartheid, and of a wide range of occupations and ages. With the exception of a few who were national leaders, they generally fulfilled the category of people who could be accurately described as second and third level regional or local leaders and organizers who were in a position to influence Black opinions. The variety of ages, occupations, education standards, and geographical locations included are important to assessing the significance (and the limitations) of this group; above all, however, it is the political representivity of the group, in proportions which accord roughly with the combined results of the three polls, which provides the principal analytical value of this sample of people.

The interviews were all carried out during a state of emergency in South Africa. This did have some effect on the research. Many of the people who should have been interviewed were detained; many were in hiding. Secondly, there were certain questions, most specifically relating to sanctions and disinvestment which were rendered illegal by legislation. In terms of the state of emergency (See Government Gazette, Regulation Gazette, No. 3964 Vol 252, No. 10280 1:vii:8c) a "subversive statement" means a statement which contains anything which is calculated to have the effect or is likely to have the effect of promoting any objective of an organization which has, under any law, been declared to be an unlawful organization, and of encouraging and promoting disinvestment or the application of sanctions or foreign action against the Republic. In the first round, questions were not asked about sanctions although many of the interviewees raised the issue themselves. Further, the nature of the questions was altered in some cases: for example, instead of asking directly whether a person supported socialism, he or she was asked whether they thought socialism was on the increase among Blacks. Further questions which might help identify the interviewee - relating to political affiliation, age and level of education achieved - were omitted. It was also not possible simply to contact potential interviewees to set up meetings. Distrust and suspicion were running high, and many would have refused interviews or given restricted replies. As a result, all interviews were arranged through intermediaries, sometimes a series of them; for every interview arranged, an average of two or three preparatory meetings were held. Everyone had to be convinced that I was to be trusted, that anonymity would be strictly respected, that my work would not harm their cause, and that it would not be simply wasteful of their time. It was a lengthy but necessary process. The responses I received indicated that the essential trust was present. Interviewees were very candid. They may well have had their own private agenda: some may have been trying to send a message to the US and the Reagan Administration; although they were requested to answer in their personal capacities some may have felt a responsibility to represent the views of their organizations; some may have been avoiding divisions within their own organizations. I have no doubt that their answers were honest: they were frank and assertive, and with very few exceptions, articulate and determined to explain their opinions carefully. This conformed to their mood.

Interviews generally lasted from one and a half to two hours; a few were shorter, a few longer. They were structured, but open-ended, and conducted as in-depth interviews rather than as a survey. Explanations, analyses and the construction of arguments were regarded as important as the actual conclusion. This meant that in many cases there was insufficient time to deal with all questions. This explains the varying numbers asked the different questions. It was felt that the research would come closer to an accurate reflection of attitudes if carried out over two years. In the second round of interviews, carried out in 1987, most questions were repeated and some questions were added. To make time for the additional questions, a few from the previous year were omitted. The structure of the second round of interviews with the 17 people who were visited in both years was as follows: They were asked ten of the questions from the first round. These were used for purposes only of comparing their answers to test for changing attitudes over the two years - this is discussed in the final chapter - and were not included in the calculations of the 1987 results. They were also asked the new questions and their responses to these are included in the 1987 results.

The timing of the two rounds of interviews is of significance. The steps outlined in the section of this chapter on the build up of Black opposition seemed to be approaching a climax in the period preceding the first round. So many pressures had been building up. Their variety was equalled only by their persistence, and by the readiness on the part of Blacks to make sacrifices. The White Government appeared to be in serious trouble. Its responses were confused; a mixture of reform and repression; reactive, now, rather than proactive. Something, it seemed, had to give. That was 1985 through early 1986. For Black South Africans this was a very exciting period. Just before the first round of interviews took place, the Government decreed the state of emergency already referred to. While many people suffered imprisonment and torture inside and outside of prison, the full impact had not yet been felt. There was still a mood of strong optimism amongst the people interviewed.

By the time of the second round, a year later, the full power of the State had been brought to bear to crush Black organizations, activism and opposition. It had not succeeded completely, but it had definitely managed to blunt the thrust of the challenge. The rising revolution had been delayed. There was consequently less optimism and excitement; more of a mood of reassessment as people cast about for new strategies.

Many of these questions have never been put on a systematic basis to Black South Africans. Their responses therefore provide unique and exciting material. At least one of the purposes of the Study is also unique; that is to bring Blacks in South Africa, and their concerns and perspectives, into the field of international relations. This has been until now a White-dominated field of endeavor with a concentration on the foreign policy concerns of the White ruled state. There was a great deal of insight, wisdom and detailed analysis contained in the answers to the questions. A further purpose of this project is to convey to those in the United States and the West who may care, the kinds of pressures that build up, and the nature of the political and strategic debates that take place, when those who have been long oppressed challenge their oppressors, and the way in which attitudes toward, and perceptions of, the US evolve in this kind of situation.

This is essentially a record: of the content and texture of debate among Black South Africans, as expressed in their own words. It is indeed a lively debate. They too are responsible for most of the analytical content in this Study. I have not attempted to reanalyze South African politics here. My role is to explain the purpose of the Study, to provide a background and context, to add short explanatory comments and summaries where necessary, and to draw conclusions from the material. My major and central task, however, in the pages that follow, is to report the responses accurately.

NOTES

1. Tom Lodge, *Black Politics in South Africa since 1945* (London: Longmans, 1983), p. 321.

2. Gavin Lewis, *Between the Wire and the Wall. A History of South African 'Coloured' Politics* (Cape Town: David Philip, 1987), p. 278.

3. John Kane-Berman, *Soweto: Black Revolt, White Reaction* (Johannesburg: Ravan, 1978), p. 48.

4. Lodge, pp. 322, 325.

5. Lodge, p. 327.

6. Eddie Webster, *Cast in a Racial Mould. Labour Process and Trade Unionism in the Foundries* (Johannesburg: Ravan, 1985), p. 127.

7. Webster, p. 128.

8. *Weekly Mail*, Johannesburg, (July 10-16 1987): 14.

9. Tom Lodge and Mark Swilling, "The Year of the Amabuthu," *Africa Report*, 31, 2 (1986): 4.

10. Andre Roux and Kirk Helliker, *Voices from Rini*, (Grahamstown: Institute of Social and Economic Research, Rhodes University, Development Studies Working Paper No. 23, 1986).

11. Roland White, "A Tide has Risen. A Breach has Occurred: Toward an Assessment of the Strategic Value of Consumer Boycotts," *South African Labour Bulletin*, 11, 5 (1986): 91-92.

12. Thomas Karis, "South African Liberation: The Communist Factor," *Foreign Affairs*, 65, 2 (1986): 267-87.

13. Merle Lipton, *Capitalism and Apartheid. South Africa 1910-1984* (Aldershot: Gower/Maurice Temple Smith, 1985), p. 347.

14. Mark Uhlig, "The Coming Struggle for Power," *The New York Review* (February 2, 1984): 28-29.

15. Lewis, p. 279.

16. Lewis, pp. 281-282.

17. Lewis, p. 282.

18. Gwendolyn Carter, Gail Gerhart and Thomas Karis, *From Protest to Challenge. A Documentary History of African*

Politics in South Africa 1882-1962, Volume 3 (Stanford: Hoover, 1977), pp. 506-539.

19. Lodge, pp. 350-351.

20. Lodge, p. 351.

21. *Clarion Call*, 4 (1985): 6.

22. See *Clarion Call*, 2 (1986): 14-17.

23. *Weekly Mail* (July 10-16, 1987): 17.

24. *Ibid.*

25. Joe Foster, Keynote Address, FOSATU Congress (April 1982), in Denis Macshane, Martin Plaut and David Ward, eds. *Power! Black Workers, their Unions and the Struggle for Freedom in South Africa* (Nottingham: Spokesman, 1984), pp. 148 and 149.

26. Cyril Ramaphosa, (Interview), *Africa Report*, 31, 2 (1986): 12.

27. *Weekly Mail* (July 17-23, 1987): 3.

28. *South African Labour Bulletin*, 11, 5 (1986): 35.

29. *Cosatu Resolutions*, February 1986 (Dalbridge: Cosatu), p. 7.

30. (Interview), *Africa Report*, 31, 2 (1986): 17.

31. Roux and Helliker, pp. 9 and 11.

32. Uhlig, p. 31.

33. Oliver Tambo, Message of the National Executive Committee of the African National Congress (January 8, 1986): 12 and 13.

34. Oliver Tambo, "Racism, Apartheid and a New World Order," *Third World Quarterly*, 8, 3 (1986): xix.

35. Tom Lodge, "The African National Congress in South Africa, 1976-1983," *Journal of Contemporary African Studies*, 3, 1/2 (1984): 176.

36. Uhlig, p. 29.

37. Lewis, p. 182.

38. David Lewis, "Capital, the Trade Unions, and the National Liberation Struggle," *Monthly Review*, 37, 11 (1986): 42-46.

39. Lipton, p. 11.

40. Neville Alexander, *Sow the Wind. Contemporary Speeches* (Johannesburg: Skotaville, 1985), p. 142.

41. Quoted in Lodge, 1984, p. 163.

42. John Saul, "South Africa: The Crisis Deepens," *Monthly Review*, 37, 11 (1986): 37.

43. "Soviet Policy in Southern Africa," *Work in Progress*, 48 (1987): 7.

44. *Weekly Mail* (July 17-23, 1987): 3.

45. Karis, pp. 394-395.

46. Uhlig, p. 29.

47. Uhlig, pp. 29-30.

48. Karis, p. 396.

PERSONAL ASSESSMENTS OF U.S. POLICY

a) THE SIGNIFICANCE OF US POLICY

QUESTION: In your opinion, is the US of significance to South Africa? In other words, do US policies and actions have a significant impact on what happens here?

Asked - 58; Yes - 53 (91% of those asked); No - 2; Conditional - 3; Don't know 0.

Will it make any difference? In the US, the actual importance of US policy to South Africa is much debated. Those who oppose an activist policy against Pretoria tend to play down its significance, pointing out that South Africa draws investment and trades with so many other countries that there are very real limitations on US influence. American anti-apartheid activists, on the other hand, would argue that it does have considerable potential for making an impact on the situation, although the more realistic among them would probably acknowledge the limitations. "Importance" is clearly not some static objectively quantifiable notion: it is a mixture of symbolism and substance, actual and potential, and relates at least to some extent to the ideological bent, acknowledged or not, which any observer brings to the subject. Amongst Black South Africans it relates to the way in which they assess the nature and source or sources of their oppression.

For 91% of this group of Black South Africans there was no doubt: the US is extremely important to South Africa. Only two of the people who were asked disagreed with this. Various explanations were given for the assessment that the US was significant. First, the US is seen as a world power, "*the* world superpower," "the most important power in the world with the economy, the resources and the clout" to make an impact if it chose to do so. "They could halt the evil if they wanted to." Second, the US holds itself out, and is seen by many in the world, as the "leader of the free world," with a commitment to freedom of speech, association and to human rights and, therefore, by committing its power to these principles in South Africa, it could have a very marked exemplary influence on other Western governments, notably the UK, West Germany, and Japan. Third, and also as leader of the free world, it could do more than any other government to deny the South African Government's long-standing claim that it is part of the Western, Christian civilized world and therefore deserves protection by the West. The US was seen as having "swallowed" this argument. Fourth, it was agreed that while US investment and trade were very important to South Africa, they were of minimal significance to the US: it would therefore not be much of a sacrifice for the US to take economic actions against Pretoria. Fifth, there was a strong feeling that despite symbolic rhetorical criticism of the South African Government, Pretoria had a strong sense of security about US intentions towards it. A number of people referred to "the conspiracy" between the two. Sixth, the US has the potential to give a substantial boost to the morale of Black people in South Africa: by isolating and weakening the South African Government, and at the same time identifying with their cause, America could strengthen the resolve of Black South Africans in what is going to be a very bitter struggle. Finally (and on a different tack), it was pointed out that the US has the potential to affect not only the Black-White struggle, but also the way in which Black politics evolves as the turbulence continues. This process was seen as already in play through US aid programs and the training of Black South Africans (the future leadership) in the US.

b) PERSONAL ASSESSMENT OF THE REAGAN ADMINISTRATION'S POLICIES

QUESTION: What is your personal assessment of the present [that is, Reagan] US Administration's policies toward South Africa? (In the second round, interviewees were asked to limit their response to the period up to mid-1986, that is the period before the changes in US policy took place.)

Asked - 93; Negative - 83 (89% of those asked); Positive - 9; Conditional - 1; Don't know - 0.

Just under 90% of those interviewed were critical, mainly very strongly so, of the Reagan Administration's policies towards South Africa. Most of the very limited approval came from members of Chief Buthelezi's Inkatha. Quoting one of them:

> Constructive Engagement is necessary for the wellbeing of South Africa at present. I'm supportive of the American Government's policy towards South Africa. Its success may not be obvious, but surely it has had an influence. South Africa listens. We oppose sanctions very actively. The US supports our view. Reagan does understand South Africa.

The other Inkatha members felt let down by the US because it was not giving their movement the recognition and support they felt it deserved. They saw this as confused in that Washington was giving aid and scholarships to people who oppose their policies, rather than to its supporters. But the general response of Inkatha, which favors Constructive Engagement, represents a deep divide from the rest of the people interviewed. A middle-level manager whose work involved the supervision of workers and who claimed to identify closely with workers also agreed with the policy.

> I agree with it. Things are very difficult as a worker. I would have a very different outlook if I were a businessman. The American Government was on a policy of Constructive Engagement but there were no tangible political results. But it did mean jobs. Certainly uneducated workers would not understand a leader of theirs who wanted changes in this. You cannot tell people they must suffer any more - it doesn't go down well.

Taken overall, however, the response amounted to an extremely broad and strong condemnation of President Reagan's policies, and it was for the most part expressed in very bitter and angry terms. Many of the first round interviews were undertaken fairly soon after President Reagan's July 1986 speech in which he indicated that Blacks in South Africa had brought some of the recent troubles down on themselves. Bishop Tutu described this talk as "nauseating" and it certainly annoyed a number of interviewees. "It is the most wicked policy ever from an American leader," commented one young professional manager. "South Africa's record of killing and torture is getting as bad as Hitler's (the speaker took trouble to explain that his numbers included deaths from malnutrition in the Bantustans/homelands), "and the US supports this," was the comment of an older, more senior man. A middle-aged woman professional explained her feelings:

> They support the South African Government. Constructive Engagement is interpreted by the South African Government as being support - it can do whatever it pleases in local and foreign affairs. Crocker never spoke to a Black South African, except maybe a few handpicked people. It looks like a policy worked out with Whites. Also, at the UN they veto anything against South Africa, and South Africa knows it can rely on them. That is why the South African Government has not moved on Namibia. The American Government does not care about Black people in South Africa.

"Constructive Engagement", as the US administration characterized its approach to South Africa, was severely criticized, as was its architect, US Secretary of State for Africa, Chester Crocker. It was described as a policy which was developed without consultation with, and therefore insulting to, Black South Africans; as giving comfort to the South African Government; as having retarded the liberation of the country; and as having failed in regard to both domestic and regional questions, such as Namibia and Angola. (The interviews were carried out before the peace talks on Namibia had made any progress.)

President Reagan was denounced from a number of different perspectives. His ability to understand the issue was questioned. "I am surprised that a respectable and sophisticated country can have him for a President.... I thought a President should be a bright, educated person," an academic councillor commented. "He has carried over the drama of Hollywood to the presidential game. It is deplorable to say the least. He doesn't know what he is saying." Doubt about him knowing what his policies really were and concern as to who really wielded power were expressed by a few people. Some people charged him with being a racist who did not care about

Blacks in South Africa, the ANC, or Mandela. They also depicted him as a "selfish capitalist who stressed economic gains at the expense of South African Blacks." He was described as right-wing. In support of this, a research worker in his 30's viewed Reagan's war-mongering talk of "Star Wars" and his plan to militarize space as "scary stuff," and also noted US intervention in Nicaragua, Grenada, and Lebanon as proof of this. Reagan was further attacked for his extreme capitalism. A journalist described him as the "Ayatollah of capitalism," as selfish, self-centered and caring only for his own capitalist system: "seen from South Africa, this capitalist system dehumanizes the poor and the rich get richer."

A number of people, mainly Azapo supporters, students, and young respondents, but also some UDF supporters, defined the policy in terms of imperialism:

> It is imperialistic. South Africa is tied by the apron strings of America, politically and economically - although this is sometimes in a complicated and subtle way. South Africa is in Angola because the US wants it to be there and knows what is going on. Actually, America is pulling the strings on the subcontinent and destabilizing it. The attacks on Zimbabwe and Zambia please the US. They are supportive of it.

Others were prepared to acknowledge that the Reagan Administration wanted some kind of change in South Africa, but this was not the kind of change Blacks wanted. It excluded any basic economic and social change and any threat to the American sphere of influence. "All they are prepared for is the White ruling class to be exchanged for Blacks incorporated into the same ruling class."

A businessman had a different, but equally hostile response to Constructive Engagement. He expressed disillusionment over the failure of the US to provide any financial assistance to Black businessmen to help them advance and more specifically to take over from disinvesting companies. He claimed that the US, in justifying its approach, had made these promises of support to Blacks operating in the private sector, but had failed to deliver. Of course, had the US furnished help to this particular group, it would have been severely criticized by others for attempting to coopt the Black bourgeoisie.

c) REAGAN'S REASONS

Asked why they thought President Reagan pursued the policies he did in South Africa, the most common response related his policies to the economic interests of the US: profits, investments, minerals, business and imperialism. The second most common answer (often combined with the first) put it down to the East-West superpower conflict and Reagan's "fear," "opposition," "obsession" with communism, socialism, and the Soviet Union. A middle-aged man, sympathetic to a democratic socialist future for South Africa, incorporated some of these points and broadened the analysis to include the southern African region:

> It is about the world spheres of influence. In the long-run, in the southern African situation, it is a struggle for the control of capital - the means of production - between two social systems, and the Reagan Administration sees it in that light. Changes here will threaten to cause social upheaval in neighboring countries and affect East-West relations. The US wants to keep the region in the fort. International capital knows that there must be change- else there is a threat of great fundamental change beyond South Africa's borders. So Western governments want to broaden the social base of South African Government but this is to stem the tide of possible fundamental social change.

The third most commonly used explanation concerned Reagan's racism. Based on his statements and actions in the US, a number of people concluded that he was a racist. ("He has no feeling for Black people or poor people.") No one seemed to argue, however, that it was pure racism that drove his policies; but rather that his sympathies for White people and his preconceptions about Black people (which were strengthened by the type of information he was getting, and his lack of understanding of the Black struggle and the reasons for Blacks resorting to violence) led him to believe that strategically and economically White rule was in the interests of the US. As one professional man said, "Kith and kin and race and profit are closely intertwined in his policies. He has a sense that Whites will be more protective of capitalism. As a minority who never allowed any other group to share, they have proved their opposition to socialism. He believes that Blacks will create a tyranny." A young community organizer explained:

> Reagan is a racist. His whole policy is based on a preconception about Black people. So he supports Whites. White people always support Whites. Just like 18th- and 19th-century colonists like Rhodes. He will say Whites stood by us in the Second World War but forgets that the very people [in South Africa] who opposed this [anti-German] alliance are in power now. He wants to ensure a supply of critical minerals and believes if Blacks take over we would be under Soviet tutelage. He sees White government as pro-West and thinks we would be Soviet puppets.

There were a few people who expressed some understanding of his reasoning. A couple of people from Inkatha, who supported his policies, believed that he was interested in the liberation of Blacks and that he was quite right "not to pretend to be the savior of somebody else." "If he forces change it won't work. It's not his job." A woman academic, who strongly opposed his policies, nevertheless acknowledged that in the real world it was natural for him to be more interested in the economic interests of the American people. And a senior executive in the private sector said that his policy of Constructive Engagement was well-intentioned. "He tried to make use of the carrot rather than the stick." However, he concluded, "he should now realize that it does not work."

d) THE 1985 SANCTIONS

Very few of the people questioned felt that the 1985 sanctions introduced by President Reagan were of any significance. A banker argued that it had made a difference in that it amounted to a warning signal to commerce and industry and they were taking action as a result; but, he went on, it had no effect on the Government. An undergraduate who acknowledged that the President had taken these steps only because Congress had pressed him, felt that such broad-based Congressional pressure was important and provided a lesson for other Western countries.

For the most part, however, it was seen as cynical and meaningless. Some quotes: "These sanctions were to preempt worse sanctions - it blunted the sanctions of the House of Representatives and the Senate." "It was a trick to delay the liberation of this country." It was symbolic." "Computers aren't going to be useful to South Africa in fighting a war against stones, rocks, etc." "The army always has access to computers and computer technology through private companies. Private companies and the SA Defense Force are intertwined- an example is ARMSCOR." And finally, a woman expressed skepticism and exasperation with the whole process: "I believe half of what it says, and of the other half I doubt it is true. It's propaganda. If it's true I don't know if it gets done. People have been deceived for a long time."

e) GROWING PERSONAL ANTAGONISM TOWARD THE US

QUESTION: Do you feel that your attitude to the US has changed in recent years? If you think back ten years or so, and reflect on how you saw the US then, and compare it with your assessment now, have you become more antagonistic?

Asked - 87; Yes - 59 (68%); No - 26; Conditional - 2; Don't know - 0.

About 70% of the group felt that they had become more antagonistic towards the US. This percentage underestimates the extent of the trend to greater hostility, because about a third of those who said no explained that they had "always" disliked the US: "To be realistic I don't see a difference now. I never liked America and I never will until it changes to meet the interests of the majority in South Africa." Along slightly different lines, a few people said that they had not become more critical but that they understood America's objectives more clearly. A university lecturer explained:

> Twelve years ago I was heavily into Black Consciousness, and we saw America as out to achieve imperialistic purposes. My change is that I now have a more sophisticated understanding. I don't dislike the Government more; I understand the content of its agenda better. It is aimed at the expansion of American capitalism. I used to see them as being interested in political control. Now I see it as neo-colonial with mainly economic motivation.... Our oppression is to further their economic interests.

A few people simply said they hated Reagan, not America; a few others acknowledged the complexity of American politics. "I distinguish the American Government and the 'extra-parliamentary movement' in the US which is a strong and effective lobby able to curtail the right-wing excesses of the Reagan Administration." Yet these were a very small minority.

Younger people talked of their primary and early high school days and the very attractive and positive image of the US which was carried in their textbooks and by their teachers, and by news of America's technological and space advances. They also acknowledged the importance to them of US fashions in clothes and music. A young trade union organizer explained:

> My background was totally exposed to propaganda. In school, bourgeois values are thumped into your head, especially junior high school ... you support the US and everything that is good comes out of the US; and there is a grave threat from the Soviet Union; and America was a knight in shining armor. Slowly, through exposure to brutality in South Africa and an understanding of the US links with South Africa, I've seen through the facade. Reading helped; and also exposure to young activists in youth organizations. We also looked at American attitudes towards Nicaragua and Angola and Vietnam and this influenced us.

A number of respondents, both young and old, mentioned that America's actions in other countries had angered them-this was not only about South Africa. This seemed to be more common in the second round of interviews. Angola was mentioned a number of times, but so too were American action in Nicaragua and the Middle East, and for two people, America's threat to world peace: "Today we see America as the biggest threat to world peace. Black people don't fall for the line that Russia is a threat, particularly since Gorbachev came to power." An Azapo official was the only person to point to the use by the US of the World Bank and the International Monetary Fund as instruments of last resort to force countries whose policies did not suit the US to change those policies. A young man working with a non-governmental education organization pointed to his own disappointment with developments in the US itself:

> Ten or fifteen years ago I looked up to America. My own political career began because of reading Martin Luther King Jr. and the Black Panthers, and we had a sense that America had dealt with and solved its problems. Now we read and know that there is still poverty and discrimination and we know that the Americans seem to ignore it. Also, we know that Americans take huge profits out of other countries and the American people don't know this. They believe what their leaders tell them.

Treatment of the American Indians came up only twice in this discussion. A young Black Consciousness advocate was concerned about the impact of American values on Black South Africans. In his view, "cultural imperialism" encourages a respect for the US and its values. Not only do these values place too much emphasis on fashions, cars, dress and consumer demands, but they have done nothing to alleviate suffering, and they take you away from your own people: they draw you away from your family and helping at home. BC ideology, he explained, stresses the importance of traditional, authentic African society and its values and the need to let Africans work out their own responses and directions. A different kind of concern, expressed by a young ANC supporter, was the penchant for US assistance to weaken and divide Black resistance. He spoke of the tremendous unity and excitement of the 1976 resistance and how the unity had been diluted through US corporate and Government money filtering into all kinds of Black projects and into the Urban Foundation and the South African College of Higher Education (Sached), and the resultant co-option of young leaders out of the mainstream of the struggle. "They intervened," he said, "because they were worried that the economy would be crippled."

Older people, too, expressed growing disappointment. They related this to their high expectations deriving from their perceptions of the civil rights movement in the US, and statements by leaders like Kennedy and Carter. An older, senior person in the UDF spoke of the American Civil War to free slaves, of the Republican President who was instrumental in ending slavery, of the hopes raised by Marcus Garvey and Dr. Aggrey, of the twenties and thirties when Black South Africans believed that the US (and Britain) would somehow rescue them because they believed the US was opposed to oppression and for the underdog. "To find a Republican Party (that is, Lincoln's Party) President protecting a system which he himself describes as abhorrent on account of its denial of rights, is something only explained in terms of economic interest, not on the basis of right and wrong." Another important figure in the UDF, confirmed his, and others, growing frustration and anger:

> Yes. All progressives in South Africa are increasingly anti-US. At mass meetings the surest way of getting applause is to hit at America. We see it as substantially supporting the South African regime. This is supported by lots of evidence from past American history. America has never supported a true liberation movement - one aimed at creating jobs, broadening education, assisting women, increasing income and welfare of all, etc. I don't think they ever supported a liberation movement except at the last minute to suit their interests.

Finally, a senior trade unionist during the second round said that his union no longer had a "Yankee go home" policy. Instead, the Unions had become more subtle in dealing with the Americans in order to advance the position of their workers. He said that visiting Americans had come to understand and respect local Black protocols better and that Blacks were now able to "use" them and influence their opinions rather than the other way around. "We used to interpret 'contact' as support. Now we accept that we can have contact and that does not mean support for the US."

To sum up, the responses contained in this chapter on personal assessments demonstrate an overwhelming hostility to US policies toward South Africa and a consequent very broad sense of growing and deepening disappointment and resentment toward the US. The US was clearly seen as a relevant factor in their continued oppression. The question was not unpackaged: it was left to the interviewees to distinguish between the Administration and "the US." Only a few did. They saw Reagan's policies toward South Africa as driven by a combination of economic self-interest, anti-communism and racism. With the exception of the Inkatha representatives, the opposition to the US covered all other categories of people from businessmen to unionists, old and young, pro-private sector and pro-socialist. Reasons may have differed, but the sentiments did not.

DISTINGUISHING BETWEEN THE DEMOCRATIC AND REPUBLICAN PARTIES

a) DIFFERENCES BETWEEN THE TWO PARTIES

QUESTION: Do you see a meaningful distinction - in regard to their policies toward South Africa - between the Republican and the Democratic Parties?

Asked - 81; Yes - 27; No - 29 (43% of those who gave an answer); Conditional - 11; Don't know - 14.

As has been explained, it was left to the interviewees to decide if they wanted to deal with "America" or break it up into components such as the President, Congress, the two parties, and the people. As can be seen so far, very few people did this. To test whether this conglomerating of "America" was an oversight, or based on lack of familiarity with the complexities of American society, or whether it was based more on some analytical framework which sees ruling class interests in the US as being essentially unified, the group was asked a series of questions relating to differences between the Democratic and Republican Parties.

Clearly, a high percentage (83%) was reasonably familiar with the two-party structure and had a sense of what the parties were about. This was higher in the 1987 interviews, which would follow from the increased attention given in the US Congress to South Africa in the second half of 1986, for example, over the sanctions legislation. Surprisingly though, the percentage of people who saw a difference decreased in the second round. The responses overall revealed an almost equal division between those who saw a meaningful distinction and those who did not, and included a good number of conditional answers.

Those who felt there was a meaningful difference made the following types of comments about the Democrats: "They are slightly to the left of the Republicans." "They are less self-centered." "They are more ready to put pressure on South Africa." "They are more sympathetic and understanding of Black South Africans." Only one person, a professional manager, criticized the Democrats. He felt that their recent proposals were too strong and that Representatives Solarz and Gray were being "too dramatic." Presumably, some Inkatha members may also have had similar criticisms, but they did not mention them. For the rest, those people who saw a difference were strongly supportive of the Democratic Party. A businessman in his early 40's, said:

> I would be very pleased if a Democrat came to power next time. Most American people have some abhorrence of racism in South Africa. If a Democrat became President he could initiate legislation against South Africa. He might show the big stick. The Democrats would not hesitate to move against South Africa.

A manager in a service organization echoed this:

> Carter was much better. The image of Democrats was better. The US image is now wicked. The South African Government would need to be careful if a Democrat came to power. There is a far difference between the two. I'm crossing my fingers that the Democrats win the next election. I hope so deeply.

By contrast, Azapo people and more left-wing elements of UDF argued that any differences between the two parties were meaningless, certainly in terms of South Africa's needs. A professional responded:

> My experience, plus my socialism and my UDF and [earlier political activity] provide my view on this. Fundamentally, no matter who is in power in the US, I have serious problems with the American approach. I met Carter appointees who made much of the change in American politics and attitudes to human rights. Yet my suspicion is always there. Their basic objective is still to see a world determined solely by American interests. It's an obsession. Americans have a crude obsession with communism. This has reached a ridiculous form now. They will sacrifice anything to fight communism.

Essentially, those who claimed there was no distinction agreed that personalities were more important than parties, that both parties were capitalist, both had to serve the interests of the "money makers"/"oligarchy"/ "big business" and, therefore, both ultimately served the same end.

There were other answers that amounted to a mixed response. A few people acknowledged that the rhetoric was different but suspected that the Democrats were mainly making a noise: it was the posturing of an opposition party which would not put these changes into practice when it took power. While this is what they thought at the time, some were ready to wait and see. A trade unionist noted that the more liberal elements of the Democratic Party were concerned with human rights, but that nobody was concerned with exploitation of workers. An Azapo supporter made the point that "democracy" means different things to different people and their (that is, the Democrats') democracy was very different from the democracy the Third World needs and was therefore of no relevance to the liberation struggle. Finally, a Johannesburg journalist, who observed a limited difference, felt that what Black South Africans were now looking for rendered the difference irrelevant. "So we are not looking for another Carter. We expect much more."

One sub-theme which emerged from more radical analysts in the 1987 interviews was that however narrow, even meaningless, the differences between the two parties were in general, nevertheless, at this particular moment in the struggle, those differences could have an impact. There was a feeling that it would be easier to build up international support for their cause if a Democrat were in power. In addition, they felt that the Namibian and Angolan conflicts might follow, what they thought would be, more constructive paths. A trade union organizer conceded:

> It does have some implication for all of our struggles in Africa.... The more liberal perspective as manifested in the Democratic Party would sort of facilitate change in this country - at least to the extent of not supporting measures supported by Ronald Reagan such as lifting the Clarke amendment on Angola. It will make it easier for the struggle here.

b) MEANINGFULNESS/SINCERITY OF CARTER'S HUMAN RIGHTS POLICY AND THE APPOINTMENT OF ANDREW YOUNG.

It is central to an understanding of Black attitudes to the US that the Reagan Administration coincided with this critical time in Black South Africa's history. It was therefore of

---

QUESTION: Do you think that President Carter's Human Rights policy was sincere and meaningful?

Asked - 39; Yes - 17 (44%); No - 10; Conditional - 4; Don't know - 8.

QUESTION: Do you think that President Carter's appointment of Andrew Young as his Ambassador to the United Nations was sincere and meaningful?

Asked - 34; Yes - 17 (50%); No - 11; Conditional - 2; Don't know - 4.

These questions were asked in 1986 only.

---

importance to find out how people felt about the Presidency of Jimmy Carter, for a favorable impression of Carter would tend to mean a more open attitude toward the US, and a recognition of the possibility of change in US policy towards South Africa. Of significance too is the fact that many younger Blacks did not remember further back than Ronald Reagan, and they said so in these interviews.

For a majority of those who answered (and the ratio of older to younger respondents is higher than for most questions), but not a large majority, President Carter, his human rights policies and his appointment of Andrew Young as his UN Ambassador had left a positive impression. The most positive statement in support of Carter came from a senior UDF official.

> Carter made it quite clear that apartheid must end there and then. Andrew Young's appointment was sincere, more so because of the part he actually played. Apartheid is based on the incapacity of the Black man to be a man. So Young, representing a superpower, undermined that myth.

Others who concluded that the actual impact of Carter and Young on southern Africa was not very substantive, still felt that the gesture was sincere, supportive of their needs, a boost to their morale, and a "good message" to Black South Africans. Others again, with a slightly different emphasis, commended Carter's general sincerity but went on to say that he had failed to win support for his policies. "Carter was more of an idealist, verging on the spiritual ... but the oligarchy overwhelmed his noises." One respondent described Carter as a "noble man, who could not win support because of imperialist tendencies in the US." He saw Young's appointment as a genuine effort which had misfired because Young was not ready. "Now he would be ready because he has run a city. He won't make the same mistakes."

For his critics, Carter was all talk and tokenism. "There was no assistance of bread or weapons. He didn't do anything. Otherwise Namibia would be free." This confirmed their view that a President can't change "certain established American principles." Young's appointment was seen by these people as a symbolic repayment for solid Black American support for Carter, and as an "attempt to pull the African bloc [at the UN] away from the East." A post-graduate student commented on Young: "We don't care about his color; he will carry out whatever Americans want. American and South African Blacks are very different." Finally, two people, a journalist and a legal adviser, both of whom thought that Young's appointment was sincere, if ineffective, warned: (anticipating at that time the possible appointment of a Black Ambassador by the Reagan Administration) "A similar gesture today would not work."

c) KENNEDY'S VISIT

In 1985 Senator Edward Kennedy visited South Africa on a fact-finding mission. He found that his reception from Black South Africans was less than unanimously positive, and on a few occasions there were public demonstrations against his presence. Demonstrations against a Kennedy anywhere will attract media attention. Given his consistently liberal record in the US, opposition from South African Blacks was indeed noteworthy. In addition, there were a number of interested parties who stood to gain by publicizing these events: the South African Government, that part of the press supportive of the Government, and conservative journalists in the USA. The reasons for including a question about these events in the interviews were, firstly, to try to discover how the group saw the demonstrations and what lay behind them; and from this to learn more about how they viewed America. For example, if people see a liberal American who has regularly demonstrated his strong opposition to apartheid, as a representative of, say, imperialism in disguise, then this says a considerable amount about their attitudes to the US and the relevance to them of political differences in the US. It is also of interest, if only in a symbolic way, to contrast his visit with that of his brother Robert two decades earlier: Robert received a warm welcome from Blacks. The change would relate more to changing Black perceptions than to the views of the two Kennedys, for Edward's record on South Africa is more clearly established than Robert's was.

The question (asked only in the first round) put to the interviewees was: "What was your assessment of the demonstrations against Edward Kennedy?" Everybody agreed that Black Consciousness people were responsible for organizing the demonstrations. Many pointed out that since BC was a minority element that the demonstrations themselves did not indicate majority support for the opposition to the visit. A number of people went on to accuse the BC groups of having received assistance from the South African security forces in setting up the demonstrations. This was of course vigorously denied by Azapo supporters and seen as a vicious attempt to undermine their standing amongst Black people. An older man, on the conservative side of the UDF, gave this sort of explanation:

> This was Azapo with the help of the security forces. The Government didn't want him here because UDF invited him; and Azapo didn't want him because he was a White man; this is nothing to do with him being an American.

An Eastern Cape businessman repeated the point that BC people had instigated the actions, but added broader explanations for them having done so, and then went on to add his own criticism of the visit:

> BC groups gave problems and that's a fringe group. BC is an irritant in the struggle. It saw it had a chance to show it was anti-American, anti-imperialist, and anti-White. There was no opposition in the UDF or to the fact that Boesak and Tutu have invited him. BC is always anti-something; they are not positive about anything; that's why they don't have any programs. Also they are not consistent about being anti-American and anti-White. It is laughable. They all want to go to America. Times have changed though. We get so many visitors. We had Robert Kennedy ... nothing happened. Lots of talk, but nothing happened. John Kennedy had a good image here. By 1986 this has gone. Very little can come via guys like Kennedy.

Although it was the BC movement that organized the open opposition to Kennedy, there was clearly a broader spectrum of views opposed. A part of this was said to have its source in the fact that some of the UDF leaders, and Tutu and Boesak were mentioned a few times, made the invitation without broad consultation within the UDF itself. About half way through the first round of the research I began to ask what the interviewees themselves thought of the visit: approximately 12 of the 20 asked were opposed to it. Commencing with those who were in favor, a banker explained:

> I met him a couple of times. He is honest and sincere. Although people said he was here for personal ambition, I believe it was a good thing that he came. He can bring first-hand information to the Senate and that is a good thing.

A middle-level manager working with a private foundation also was positive about the Kennedy trip:

> It was good ... My church would welcome him. I welcome him. A small group protested and the Government gave it publicity. The Government arranged it. The BC position is pointless. Kennedy is doing more than a guy like me because he can influence Americans. So we shouldn't chase him away.

A middle-aged woman who had worked with trade unions said that she appreciated his visit because he had come to talk and it was preferable that he should learn from the "horse's mouth" than from looking at propaganda on TV. "He learnt a lot," she added.

Moving on to those who had mixed feelings, two quotes will be given; the first from a young Cosatu-affiliated union organizer:

> The struggle of Black South Africa and its workers has to be fought by ourselves, and he represents a country whose workers have been exploited. He sees the problem differently from us. Also we do not trust the Kennedys' behavior in other countries. So it is very questionable whether he wants to help. On the other hand I consider his visit was part of the increasing international momentum against South Africa, and the South African Government was not pleased. So people can try to justify this visit because it isolated the Botha regime.

The second was from a Nactu-affiliated trade union organizer:

> I saw Kennedy's visit in two perspectives. He is a representative of capital and the West with an interest inside South Africa. At the same time, I recognize him as a mover and a shaker in the Democratic Party and the Congress. He needed to hear directly from us and we therefore saw him. He is an important part of the power

> structure. We allowed Azapo to protest outside and inside the building here, but we talked to him. We recognize the right of Azapo to protest: they should recognize our right to talk to him. Democracy has two edges: to recognize and be recognized and this should be respected.

Inkatha representatives were also negative about Kennedy's visit. This is one of the few questions where they came close to coinciding with the mainstream of opinion in this group. They came to their conclusion from a different direction, however. They were not so much opposed to his visit in advance, but were disappointed in his underestimating the significance of the support for Chief Buthelezi and Inkatha, in his opposition to their movement and in his support for sanctions. According to a young Inkatha official, the visit was useless and produced nothing of value for Blacks. An Inkatha supporter, in his early thirties, working for a multinational corporation in Durban, criticized Kennedy for having "no interest in South Africa at heart," for having preconceived notions, and for "trying to tell us what to do." An older, senior Inkatha official complained:

> He had come to make his own name, to prove his support for Blacks. So he received a bad reception from Azapo. Inkatha welcomed him, but it was not a happy welcome. We wanted him to see Inkatha. He saw Mandela and we wanted him to see the following of Buthelezi. He saw it. He saw the thousands of young people supporters of Buthelezi. However, afterwards he wrote an anti-Buthelezi and an anti-Inkatha paper. He is riding the bandwagon of anti-Buthelezi sentiment.

A critic from the UDF explained his view of the visit:

> Inside the UDF too, there was a strong feeling against America and Kennedy. We used to look up to the Kennedy's as decent people, but we know now they are capitalists, and we don't want them. This view is quite strong inside the UDF, and there was division about this.

Finally, we need to turn to the views of Azapo supporters,

for it is their organizations that staged the demonstrations. To start with, a first year Azapo student felt:

> He is an agent of imperialism. He is not interested in any fundamental change in South Africa. He just wants to abolish apartheid, to enhance capitalism and his own family's interests and his chances of winning the Presidential election in 1988. Also people remember JFK when African revolutionaries were being killed by the C.I.A.

A second Azapo supporter, in his 30's, working for a church-funded, non-Governmental organization said:

> That is why we demonstrated against Kennedy - to explore by all possible means the relationship between America and South Africa as evils related to each other. If we see oppression as only Whites against Blacks we miss the broader enemy and we miss the subtle links of the oppressive system.

And a third BC supporter, this one a postgraduate research assistant in his 30's, said that it was too late for Kennedy.

> We saw ourselves being sold out by Tutu. He came from the US and that is that. I opposed him because he came from the American system and America can't help. We want liberation and political power and land - and America can't help.

d) THE IRAN-CONTRA SCANDAL

QUESTION: What are your views on the recent events in the US involving the sale of arms to Iran, the transfer of profits to the Contras in Nicaragua, and other related matters now collectively known as "the Iran-Contra scandal?"

Asked - 55; Negative - 44 (80%); Positive - 2; Conditional-0; Don't know - 6; Not interested - 3.

Fifty-five people were asked their opinions on the "Iran-Contra scandal." Of the 46 who answered (6 had no answer and 3 said they were not interested) two came up with something positive to say, and this related to the openness of the investigation. The rest (96%) were very critical; contending that it revealed insincerity and duplicity in US policy, and a willingness to intervene in third world countries whenever they deemed it in their interest to do so. One positive assessment came from a senior trade union official in Johannesburg:

> After Angola and Savimbi we are not surprised at all to see them trying to buy influence; and politics does make for strange bedfellows. However, what is important there is that the whole American system is an open system; this is very different from a political scandal in the USSR-one needs to bear that in mind. Also it is a lesson to us here where we have commissions of enquiry which don't investigate anything. We need to think of their open system and compare it with the Langa Enquiry and enquiries here about Black-White issues.

Another favorable comment came from a unionist in Cape Town. While this man saw Reagan as "a petty gangster," he was impressed by "their bringing it all out in the open. Britain would keep it quiet. But we do wonder what we don't know about." The rest were unconditionally critical. Some of the responses dealt with the President himself. A university lecturer concluded that Reagan was guilty, and that there was a major attempt to protect him, the Presidency, and the Republican Party. "I can't understand how he gets away with 'I can't remember'; particularly so if you look at his speeches of support for the Contras." A researcher expressed concern that Reagan had lost control and did not know what was going to happen next. "Is he a front or a person in control?" An adviser working with a voluntary agency said that it demonstrated the President's double standards: "His stated policy is not to deal with Iran, but when it suits his needs he does."

A second type of response dealt with ways in which this reflected on the American political system. A woman administrator in an advisory organization said in this regard that it confirmed her in her view that America would disrupt, and perpetuate divisions among, other countries in its own interest. For a woman academic it furnished confirmation that the system was corrupt: "It is like a body with boils. You don't know where the boils will pop up next." A professional man in Cape Town commented:

> It reinforces our impression that the rhetoric about supporting democratic countries repeated constantly to us by the US is false. The US will support non-democratic and reactionary and tyrannical movements like the Contras and the MNR [in Mozambique]. They keep doing it.

A trade unionist, referring to Oliver North and his appearance before a commission of enquiry concluded:

> It is farcical. The primary perpetuator is hailed as a hero even though he is dismissed by the President. He is given the status of a hero. The politicians become prostitutes, even some of the people on the investigation commission. They are swinging to the side of public opinion to keep their popularity.

A third group of answers made some parallel or connection with South Africa. A graduate student said:

> These are again some of the issues we take into account when we assess America, even though these countries are far away.... We want to see people in Nicaragua as friends because these people are facing oppression by the Western powers. When we see the American Government using dollars to finance Contras, we look harder at those dollars for Black education in South Africa. Our friends in Nicaragua are being blown to pieces by the very same dollars. We look at these contradictions and it breeds hostility to the US.

A trade union official saw a parallel in the South African State Security Council making - even dictating - policy to the White elected Parliament which had not appointed it and to which it was not responsible. This was particularly the case on security legislation and decisions on cross-border raids. "They have learnt good lessons from America. America probably has a hand in the South African offensives and South Africa assists in American interventions in various parts of the world." A manager thought that the affair might dent Reagan's popularity, and, he hoped for the sake of Blacks in South Africa, that as a consequence people in America would stop supporting him. An Inkatha supporter found it incomprehensible that Reagan did not know all about it. "It left me wondering if they might be pumping money into the South African Defence Force and if one day we will learn about that." A public interest lawyer said that the affair epitomized America's stance: "They are ready to counter by any means what they see as communist influence. They are not different from South Africa when it comes to communism. So they will always be pro-South Africa."

As the most publicized domestic issue of late 1986/ early 1987, the Iran-Contra scandal has most certainly harmed still further an already negative evaluation of US - and Republican Party - foreign policy. It must also have damaged the perceptions of the US political system itself. Its one possible redeeming feature - the openness of the investigations - attracted positive comments from only a couple of people. It was also clear that the Black South Africans represented here were well pleased that Reagan, whom they saw as opposing their cause, might have lost credibility and support as a result.

e) THE NOVEMBER 1986 US ELECTION

Elections in America's off year - that is when the Presidency is not at stake - would attract limited attention in South Africa. This question was nevertheless included to further test attitudes to the Democratic and Republican Parties.

Partly because of time constraints during interviews, and partly because it was assumed that some of the interviewees would not be familiar with the outcome, the question was put to only 42 members of the second round group. Of these, 15 were aware of the results, and of these 15, 12 were pleased, one was not, and two felt that the results were irrelevant to South Africa. The one person who was disappointed was an Inkatha member:

> We are not pleased with the results. The Democrats did well because they are in favor of sanctions. They think it can change South Africa; as it is it won't change anything.

The rest who were familiar with the results and felt they were relevant to South Africa were pleased. A trade unionist was encouraged: "Things changed dramatically. We saw that the Democrats' position had improved and that this might mean a growing swing away from the conservatives." A medical doctor also expressed pleasure: "It is a move away from Reagan. It may change American policies towards South Africa, and also increase the chances of international peace." Two interviewees, whose analysis led them to see little difference between the two parties, nevertheless felt that "within the present context" of the South African situation and of US-South African relations, that results favoring the Democrats did make a difference and they too were pleased.

Without any doubt these Black South Africans would have voted overwhelmingly for a Democratic candidate in the Presidential election. (At the time of the interviews the likely candidates were unknown.) While President Reagan personally was seen as extremely conservative and unhelpful to their cause, they also saw the Republican Party as more conservative and less helpful to their liberation than the Democrats. This sentiment was clearly expressed by many of the group. It was apparent too in the pleasure many of them took from President Reagan's troubles over the Iran-Contra scandal; and from those few who were familiar with the results of the November 1986 election in which the Democrats had made gains. For some, possibly half of the group, this was a relatively clear difference; for others, the philosophies of the two parties were seen as almost identical. Yet even many of this latter group would concede that at that particular moment in South Africa they thought a Democratic President would be of more use to them. Possibly 20-25% of the respondents felt that in the ultimate service of capitalism, the two parties were fundamentally the same. This is reflected in some of the comments on Edward Kennedy's visit. This would become even more apparent if one were discussing the possibility of radical social and economic change in South Africa which they supported, and which they felt would be opposed equally by both the Republicans and the Democrats. The general favoring of the Democrats over the Republicans is not to be equated with great optimism or deep belief in what the Democrats would actually achieve on their behalf.

ASSESSMENT OF BLACK SOUTH AFRICAN ATTITUDES TOWARD THE UNITED STATES

a) ASSESSMENT OF ATTITUDES

QUESTION: I have asked you your own personal views about the US. Now I want to ask you your assessment of Black South Africans in general. In your opinion, are Black South Africans anti-American?

Asked - 93; Yes - 75 (81%); No - 6; Conditional - 9; Don't know - 3.

QUESTION: In your opinion are Black South Africans becoming increasingly anti-American? Please think back ten years or so and compare their attitudes then with now.

Asked - 87; Yes - 68 (78%); No - 8; Conditional - 9; Don't know - 2.

"Black South Africans in general" is an ill-defined category; and it was left to the respondents to interpret as they chose. Some were ready to generalize; others spoke about communities with which they were familiar; others broke Blacks into categories and dealt with each category separately. The purpose was to get some sense of what they saw as happening to the perceptions and attitudes of Black South Africans, and their analysis of those trends. The majority (approximately 80%) answered both questions in the affirmative. Answers to these two questions were characterized by a good deal of hostility to the US.

Once again, representatives of Inkatha stood out as having a different evaluation from most of the group. An Inkatha urban official argued that Black leaders of other organizations were becoming anti-American, but this was to "keep their names up," "to retain their status among Black people," and "to get their pay packets." In general, he was of the opinion that most Black South Africans were not becoming anti-American: "Most people in the know are strongly friendly with the US. Ordinary people want investment; they do not want sanctions. They want to keep their bread." One trade union organizer felt that there was considerable support for the US because of its grants for educational programs for Blacks and church assisted community projects.

A small number made the distinction between President Reagan and "America"; that is, they thought the anger was directed at the President and not at the country and its people. A first-year student acknowledged that many people in the US showed solidarity with Black South Africans and also that the political system was very complex. By contrast, a middle aged woman professional who made the distinction, nevertheless argued that Americans should not be excluded from the blame. "We see Reagan's policy as giving the green light to the South African Government to kill, torture, oppress and invade. And we see how much the Americans like and support Reagan."

A few people pointed out that it was necessary to limit their assessments to the politicized, mainly urban people. A priest who worked in the rural areas of the Cape commented: "In the rural set-up, they are not aware of these issues." And a young Inkatha organizer argued that many urban workers were ignorant as well. "For example, there are a number of people who work for Coca-Cola who don't know whether it is an American company or not." Someone observed that, in reality, Blacks might be angry with the US, but that they were far too busy with the internal struggle to give too much attention to it. A graduate student contrasted politicized people who were angry with non-politicized people, the majority, who were still culturally and ideologically subjected to American influence, and consequently were not anti-American. While some responses indicated categories of people where anti-American feeling was less strong, others pointed to groups where negative sentiment was more advanced. For example, a middle-level manager said that young people who were more informed and more hostile were taking over - "and they see things that their fathers did not see. Ten years ago the ratio of young people to old people in politics was say 3:7; now it's 7:3." A woman lawyer singled out the trade unions in this regard: "Politics for workers means to ally with organizations to fight for liberation and a socialist society, and America is the antithesis of their goals."

A very angry man in his early thirties, a community organizer in Soweto, noted that there were some mixed feelings. On the one side, Blacks had respected the civil rights movement. Also, some day they would need "to borrow some things" from the US such as the Bill of Rights and true capitalism (as opposed to the South African version) and some decentralization. On the other side, the US had turned against them; also, they sympathized with the people of Vietnam and Nicaragua. So there was a love-hate relationship. A young man in Durban pointed to the need to distinguish between the political (in which there was increasing hostility) and the cultural spheres, where he saw empathy growing - in TV, the Cosby Show, movies, music, taste, dress.

Yet most typical was the assessment of a young professional, stated unconditionally, that there was growing antagonism towards the US:

> Since 1976 our people have been in a state of unrest and have been killed, and the USA was never seen to do anything physical to halt the situation. Our movement, which we respect, the ANC, is called terrorist, and they refuse to deal with them.

A Ph. D. student described a funeral in Queenstown where the first speaker attacked Reagan rather than Botha and other speakers kept ridiculing Reagan. "Right across the board there is great disappointment - not hatred as much as disappointment." A man employed in a trade union support agency gave this analysis:

> Twelve years ago few people even thought about it. As the struggle increased, and the open collusion between the South African Government and the US became clearer, and also America's hostility to progressive African States, so Blacks in this country became hostile. The US is an obstacle to our liberation. It used to be different. But a new generation is rising. Experience of the struggle broadens and intensifies, and the analysis changes in the process. Therefore people look at things in a different way. It is a combination of experience in the struggle and an attempt to understand what you are struggling against.

Interviewees felt that increasing animosity was a broad and strong phenomenon. When pressed to think of exceptions to this trend, they suggested Inkatha, the "independent" Bantustan leaders, possibly some members of the National African Federated Chamber of Commerce, maybe some members of the middle class; people, they suggested, "who feared real change." Lengthy comments were made in explaining why they thought Black South Africans felt hostility to the US. A representative list of typical examples follow:

> People are very critical - even of funding from the US. Three organizations in Johannesburg have just stopped accepting money to review the motives - to see if the intention is to buy them off or to help them. [A priest.]

> When Reagan won again people became very disappointed. We know we can't expect others to do it for us but we moderates hoped for help. [A middle-level manager with a trade union background.]

> It is not the line of our people to be anti-American, but the Americans have lost our respect. [A priest.]

> Reagan's speeches make it worse all the time. He shows great ignorance. [A final year student.]

> When he [Reagan] talked about the shooting of Blacks at Langa and said the police were compelled to do so, he didn't know what was going on. Also, his denial of sanctions. [A first year student, a supporter of UDF.]

> There is increasing awareness of American imperialism ... that America is the enemy. [An Azapo officeholder.]

A number of unionists, both Cosatu and Nactu sympathizers, referred to the behavior of US companies in South Africa as a further cause; but this will be discussed below. Finally, an academic made the following observation about the youth:

> Young people are striving for change; people who have fled got help from the Soviet Union, Eastern Europe, African states. Clearly no one is going to the States and Britain to seek training, and people don't look to Western Europe and America as allies in producing change. Young people are looking more and more to the East. I'm sure this is true also of trade unionists and the working class.

One additional response should be tacked on to this discussion. Skepticism about this hostility on the part of Inkatha has been mentioned. Doubts were also expressed about the reality of this anti-Americanism amongst top leaders by a graduate student, a supporter on the left of the UDF:

> Many are critical but they don't have a platform. Our leadership level is being manipulated. Tutu, on paper, attacks America but in practice he is "an American" - he is like [Zimbabwe's Bishop] Muzorewa. He strikes me as a confused priest. We are becoming increasingly critical of our leadership. Why did Tutu talk to P. W. Botha? - I don't trust it. Most African leaders have a different style of life from the masses - which is expensive. There is a growing divide from the masses. How does he earn his money? Tutu doesn't understand the poor and suffering. He is in a "paying" business. People are becoming critical of our bourgeoisie; for example, Tutu and Motlana's kids are not affected by Bantu education. Politics is a game for them; politics for the masses affects their lives.

Asking a group of people for their assessment of trends in Black opinion is of course not the same as carrying out a national survey. Also, despite the emotion expressed in many of the answers, the depth of feeling and its potential staying-power could not be easily assessed. Nevertheless, one needs to take note of the emotional content of the responses and the number of respondents who were prepared to generalize about this. Further, this was widely seen as a trend which was growing with time and experience in the struggle, and with increased politicization by the leadership; which was seen by the vast majority of this group as anti-American. One may also safely deduce from these responses (which need to be read in conjunction with those in Chapter 2) that there was growing anger - at the very least, disappointment - among politically informed and politically active Black South Africans.

RADICALIZATION

a) INCREASED RADICALISM

Chapters 2 and 4 set out to determine how this group of Black South Africans felt about the US, how they thought other Black South Africans felt about the US, and to discover reasons and explanations for their answers. The responses, analyses, terminology, and emotion have taken us some way towards understanding how Black South Africans are changing and the linkage between those internal changes and the altered perceptions of the US. Chapters 5 and 6 give attention to the way in which the group sees the dynamic of change in Black domestic politics. It does this by exploring with the in-

---

QUESTION: In your opinion, are Black South Africans becoming more radical? After they had responded, they were then asked what they meant by "radical."

Asked - 74; Yes - 64 (86%); No - 1; Conditional - 8; Don't know - 1

---

terviewees a number of aspects related to "radicalism," an essential analytical step toward gaining an insight into the bases for changing attitudes towards international issues in general and the US in particular. In order to commence this discussion, the first question was open-ended and undefined. Nearly everyone who responded felt that a process of radicalization was under way.

Possibly a third of the group who felt this was happening placed some kind of limitation on their comments. One middle-aged executive noted that while radicalism had increased among the youth, this should not be taken too seriously. "They are easily misled. Their radicalism is ill-formed and they could easily be changed." A young executive in a large private company felt that the radicalism had increased because the Government had become less strict about controlling people's public rhetoric. A businessman argued that this was despair, not radicalism: "They are not supporting leftist policies, they are just losing hope. The economic situation is contributing to despair and total helplessness. So people are trying out leftist ideas and slogans." A young Inkatha organizer felt that there was "no change in the yearning for liberty" and that people were not ready to die: "Otherwise, they'd all march into town." The only difference he saw was that the "more radical groups were ready to kill each other." And finally, a community organizer, on the left of the UDF, felt that there was definitely such a process under way but its potential seemed limited: "The youth have become incredibly radicalized in a militant sense, but they are stunted in not having access to political debates."

A number of people suggested reasons why this was happening; and the core of their case was that the people had finally been pushed into a corner and had been left with no other way out. A banker, who was clearly uncomfortable with this process at work in Black society discussed the causes:

> Yes, it is under way. It is caused by police brutality, by general repression, by the inability of the Government to show signs of will to negotiate power-sharing. Every death cuts off the links between Black and White communities. Every death affects someone. There have been massive deaths, for example, in Uitenhage and Mamelodi, and this radicalizes entire communities. There are disturbances in very remote areas of the country and it's happening in every facet of the community - church, sports, schools. The youngest of kids know Mr. Mandela and what he stands for.

Through its actions over a long period of time, Pretoria had created the circumstances on which Black radicalism must inevitably thrive. It nevertheless required initiators, articulators and organizers to evolve as it has. Three "categories" of people were identified as driving this process forward: trade unionists, "the youth" and "leaders." Trade unions, which in the last decade had made dramatic gains in organizational effectiveness and politicization, were said to have played an active role in implanting new understandings of the nature of exploitation and then testing those ideas in "radicalizing" undertakings such as consumer boycotts, strikes and stay-aways. The youth, both organized and less organized, angered and frustrated by inferior education, poor opportunities and their treatment by the Department of Education, had done much to radicalize themselves and their elders. An ex-trade union organizer observed:

> Only after the 1976 riots, when the youth took over giving out instructions. At first, their elders did not take notice of these kids. Now they have to. Through destruction they have created fear and then mobilized and conscientized. This has been done not by talk but by frightening people.

And thirdly, a vague category of "more articulate leaders" and "leaders with a better understanding of the implications of international politics" - these could be in community organizations, student organizations, trade unions, large political organizations, intellectuals - were said to be strengthening an understanding of Black circumstances, and the implications of different strategic options.

While nearly everyone agreed that a process of radicalization was taking place, there were numerous and different ideas about what this meant. For example: much more demanding; demand for total change, not reforms; militant; violent; impatient; outspoken; leftist; will stand up to dying and suffering; ready to boycott and strike; the fast growing number involved in anti-establishment activities; killing each other; we can't stand nonsense any longer; far more people on the real left than there used to be; young people can now organize at a most sophisticated level in complete secrecy.

A young community activist in the Eastern Cape described the process in this way:

> They are becoming more radical. They have come to accept that they will suffer and die for freedom. Sixteen and seventeen-year-olds go and throw stones at the military vehicles. They know they will die. And they are prepared. We have seen too much death and hurt. And we have gone a long, long way and we won't go back. And we see better what we are fighting. We know it is not the Government only. We know that we must take over the economic structures as well.

A UDF office-holder indicated how the Freedom Charter was being interpreted differently by more and more people, and how this change in interpretation indicated a movement from a liberal democratic to a socialist democratic thrust. An explanation of this will be addressed in the next chapter in the section dealing with socialism. Finally, by way of illustration, a trade unionist in Cape Town gave the following vivid description of what he understood by growing radicalism:

> It was absolutely clear at the funeral we had here on Sunday. The Government banned us from doing certain things; there were warnings in the papers. But our people disregarded these warnings. This is a change. Even five years ago, if an event was banned people wouldn't come. Now people have a total disregard for the law. In 1985, we had the Saint Athens Street Mosque incident. Students were killed. One was a Moslem. The police wouldn't release his body. So there was a protest to demand his body. Police teargassed and shot into the crowd. A young man tried to leave and he was killed by the police. The next day Athlone looked like Greece under the Colonels, or Latin America. There were amazing scenes. The army arrived and sealed off the whole area. They searched the area house by house. It was an incredible show of force. The next day there was a funeral for the boy who had been shot. A huge number of people attended. The stadium was packed and two football fields were tightly packed; and then we marched to the cemetery. The people were not intimidated. At a general level they are not intimidated by the State despite the violence, the repression, the killing. Everybody knows they can be arrested tomorrow. At funerals they are teargassed and they still demonstrate. At the mass level the legitimacy of the State has disappeared.

b) RADICALISM CONTINUED: VIOLENCE

As a next step, "radicalism" was broken into four different possible meanings, and questions were asked about each. The first related to violence; more specifically, whether there was a greater acceptance that violence was essential for purposes of bringing about change. For most of the people the answer was not only "yes," but all too obvious. Evidence all around proved it. During the second round of interviews, I spoke to a man, an hour after a major explosion had taken place in downtown Johannesburg, in an office a few blocks from where it had occurred. All around the streets were strewn with shattered glass. I asked him this question. He simply smiled and looked out the window.

QUESTION: I want now to break radicalism into four types, and ask separately about each. First, violence. Is there a greater acceptance among Blacks that some violence is essential in order to bring about change?

Asked - 58; Yes - 51 (88%); No - 4; Conditional - 3; Don't know - 0.

An elderly man, a technical assistant and community organizer all went to some length, as did a number of others, to stress that this was the forced alternative, and gave a history of peaceful attempts to bring about a change and the Government's responses. And a woman academic stressed how difficult it was for her personally to accept violence:

> It repels me. As a middle-aged parent I think about it a lot. About limbs maimed and deaths and so on. Accepting violence doesn't come easily. But the proof is in the realities, especially among the young.

A number of people pointed out that it was strongest among the young: "They won't allow themselves to suffer like their fathers and forefathers. They are prepared to die for their freedom: they will let loose whatever they have," because they have come to "believe that the only language the Government hears is violence."

A young private sector executive who supported Inkatha argued that the majority opposed violence, but acknowledged that the minority was growing: "There is an increasing market share of violence."

> What we see is sporadic violence. It goes in ups and downs. This means the majority don't like violence; otherwise it would keep going. A few people, on specific issues, get support for violence towards specific ends. A very small group can intimidate the rest of the people. It is easy to do violence. It's much harder to do good. Twenty people can do a lot of damage.

A graduate student, a supporter of ANC and UDF, made the point that violence was not always indicative of radicalism. In his view, in 1976 and soon after, Black youth were very radical politically, but their politics were now in the process of "deteriorating:" "While fighting for liberty [against the Government] would demonstrate commitment to radicalism, fighting against each other, killing each other "demonstrated a weakening of radicalism, a breaking away from the ANC."

In the course of the 1987 interviews a number of people made the point that the use of violence had in fact produced positive results. A lawyer argued that in those areas where there had been more violence there had been more improvement, and illustrated this by comparing the better education in Soweto, granted in response to violence, to the lack of change in Natal. A graduate student pointed out that when there was no violence, nothing happened, and outside countries remained unaware of what was going on in South Africa. Through violence and the police reaction to it, one could expose to the world the ills of apartheid. A young administrative officer gave a few examples:

> It stopped Afrikaans as the official language in schools. Education has improved and there has been an improvement in teacher training and in teachers. We threw stones at company cars. This put pressure on business to press the Government for change. Violence also brought unity, and eased the way for parents and kids to come together.

c) RADICALISM CONTINUED: BLACK CONSCIOUSNESS

As discussed in the Introduction, the struggle in South Africa has changed dramatically in the dozen years since 1976. It has spread fast both geographically and in terms of the categories of people participating. Organizations have multiplied at all levels. The ANC is back. The UDF has emerged. The unions have grown in strength. Ideologies are changing, evolving and being fought over. Internal divisions have grown more bitter. Black people are accusing Black people of betraying the struggle. In other words, the most readily and immediately mobilizing element in the revolution, race, is losing some of its currency. Furthermore, terms like oppression, exploitation and class conflict are theoretically color-blind and the growing number of Black officials, Black policemen, Black bourgeoisie, Black Bantustan leaders who exploit or oppress or at least benefit materially from the system has filled the ANC non-racial analysis with concrete examples to abet cogently its arguments. On the other hand, it remains true that the predominant percentage of people who are oppressors and who are beneficiaries of the system are White. In all of this, what has happened to the "BC" movement, so influential in the 70's, so central in motivating the uprisings of 1976, and so initiating the turbulence that has challenged Pretoria ever since?

QUESTION: A second possible interpretation of radicalism in the South African context relates to Black Consciousness. Do you think that Black Consciousness, as propounded by the Black Consciousness movement, is growing?

Asked - 77; Yes - 19; No - 38 (49%); Conditional - 20; Don't know - 0.

This study is based on perceptions and attitudes; as such it acknowledges the potential mix of subjectivity and objectivity in most of the answers. Possibly more than most other sets of answers this one on the influence of BC (as it will be referred to) appeared to contain a strong subjective element. In the main, BC officials and sympathizers thought it was growing in one way or another or making advances or maturing or evolving. Similarly, opponents saw its influence as steadily diminishing. Many non-BC people, however, gave conditional answers. In numerical terms, the responses amount to a clear majority of those who gave a definite answer, saying that its influence was on the wane. This is corroborated by the surveys referred to in the Introduction. Further - as will become clear in the discussion that follows - many of those who argued that its influence was on the rise also observed that it was changing its nature. Taking these observations and trends together indicates rather convincingly that BC as it manifested itself in the 1970s has reduced significantly in importance. (The percentage of people who argued that it was on the decline increased noticeably during the second round of interviews.)

Not surprisingly, discussion was complex. People addressed the question from a variety of angles. A couple of respondents, despite the specific wording of the question, saw it as relating to a general enhanced level of consciousness and anger among Blacks. Some saw it as measurable in terms of support for, and membership of, BC movements such as Azapo, Azactu, and Azasm. Others saw it as a developing dynamic ideology whose alterations were directed by people associated with those organizations. Keeping this in mind, let us look first to the views of those, the majority, who felt its influence was diminishing. A few of these people acknowledged (and most of the others would probably agree) that the BC movement played a very positive role in strengthening the identity, confidence, and assertiveness of Blacks, and in stimulating the determination of the youth in the 70's. But, they argued, it had been a phase, and for a number of reasons it "was now on the wane."

> It performed its function. Progressive movements in this country are multiracial. Azapo, Azactu, and Azasm are so very small. It was a phase, like a phase of liberalism in the early 60's.
>
> It was the foundation of radicalism. That was basic to this (what we now have). "The White man won't help you. Do it yourself." Biko said this. But it is fading a bit. Your student groups were all BC. But now ANC preaches non-racialism. Which is completely different from what Biko said. BC helped us achieve confidence, but now it is antagonistic to the ANC.
>
> What do you expect to happen under racial repression? Reaction must be the opposite of White oppression. BC was no different from Afrikaner consciousness, purified Afrikaner consciousness. The English did not understand the importance of the Great Trek, the concentration camps, Blood River. PAC was like that ... Afrikaner nationalism worked. It was a lesson to some Blacks. But we are all interdependent; in the economy particularly, completely interdependent. Separation on the basis of color is not acceptable. BC is not increasing. UDF and its affiliates have proved Black separateness is not feasible.

Others went on to explain why this was occurring. Two interrelated themes emerged: a criticism of its analysis and content, and various explanations of its organizational ineffectiveness. For example, an ex-union officer in the Eastern Cape said that a racial response to White racism was not an answer. "It is racism and I don't agree with it. The thing is dead in the Eastern Cape. In Johannesburg maybe 10% support it. It has nothing going for it." A graduate student argued:

> It is a reactionary type of radicalism, if it is radical at all. It is similar to the White AWB and Terreblanche, that is, extreme racism. It came and went - it's gone. We must fight the system, not the people.

A Cosatu-affiliated union official explained:

> It has weakened since the establishment of the UDF and the reason is that people have been mobilized in a way

> that they don't see the enemy on the basis of color; and the more people develop these [non-racial] strategies, the more they see the mistakes of BC.

He went on to note that at times he understood BC and did not blame them: "It is the way Blacks are treated in this country. They [BC] use that treatment to mobilize people." A first-year student who was an Azapo supporter felt that the movement was "stuck."

> It is not going anywhere. It has been messed up by the so-called donors - churches, corporations, institutions- who don't give money to BC; only to nonracial organizations so that non-racial organizations can organize better. Also BC leadership lost credibility - and a leader was involved in crime. It is weakening not because it is meaningless but because of financial problems.

A prominent UDF personality in Johannesburg explained the weakening of the movement in the following way:

> Look back to '76. The youth revolted, they were detained; they fled the country, they felt themselves the spearhead for change. The only organization to benefit from this was the ANC. The only organization able to address the problems of the country was the ANC. And the youth saw this. They saw that BC groups could not address the problem of the transfer of power. It is the same as the various socialist groups that emerged in this country over time. They can help politicize, but they can't *do* it. They don't have the organizational strength. So some of them asked where to attach themselves most effectively. Look back to the 50's. They had to work within the framework of the national organizations. So today we see BC divided. Most are in the ANC. Some socialists, like the National Forum, thought it more effective to their cause to align themselves with BC in order to get some mass base and also increase their strength to negotiate with the Democratic Movement. That is the only new lease of life BC has had. So it is weakening. Its only strength now is its association with this particular socialist element.

A few people discussed its failure to take mass organization seriously. Even at its most effective it remained elitist and restricted to intellectuals. While its ideas had a significant influence it did not succeed in involving the people in the struggle. As a result, after 1976, when emotion was high, it did not have the capacity to translate its ideas into action.

A couple of people who agreed that BC appeared to be losing momentum interjected important questions about the real depth of the change. A Soweto community organizer explained:

> It is reducing in the intellectual field. Now we realize we need each other. But we still get frustrated because Whites always want to *dominate* [this refers to White progressive supporters controlling non-racial organizations]. And the masses down there are saying we are poor because they are rich and we are Black and they are White and we want to exchange roles.

And a woman academic agreed:

> Our politics are painfully confused. The slogan now is non-racism. But how deep it goes I don't know. Non-racial noises don't mean non-racism. And there is a problem that Whites still want to do things for us. It is very difficult to assess if BC is weakening.

She went on to give examples of multiracial tea parties organized by White women at which Black women had still felt distinctly uncomfortable and at which nothing was accomplished and which soon ceased. While she acknowledged that this was not an important example, it left her with feelings of doubt about the reality of non-racialism.

There seems little evidence to suggest that membership of BC-affiliated organizations was increasing, and BC supporters did not make their case on the basis of membership numbers. Rather they argued that the ideas of the movement were increasingly influential and were taking root in other organizations; and in addition that those ideas were in a state of evolution. A postgraduate student here explains how he saw White pressure undermining the movement and how it was nevertheless unconsciously taking root in the supposedly non-racial UDF.

> It is growing, but it has been hijacked. 1976 was spearheaded by the BC movement. It was crushed by the Boers.

> So Black youth left the country and joined the ANC and PAC. Then the progressives came up. The Freedom Charter emphasizes non-racialism. White organizations joined Black organizations in the UDF. All of these are taking over Black-initiated organizations. UDF has Whites and gets money from Whites. The White-controlled media downplays PAC because it is scared of it. PAC is closely connected to Azapo. But still the people see oppression by Whites - it is obvious. UDF still sing anti-White songs. Our people see themselves as Africans, and until we see ourselves as equal in every sphere we can't trust Whites.

The following statements indicate the directions in which four leaders of BC-oriented organizations felt the movement and its ideas were going. These are given at length because of the detail of the arguments and because they relate to, analyze and justify changes over time and changes whose outcomes are yet unclear.

> The most radical socialist program of action is the current National Forum position on these issues. They have a very clear perception of where they want to go - the stumbling block is that of US foreign policy and the Kennedy visit is a case in point. Biko and others spoke about capitalism etc, but because of the period they operated with no specific clarity. Saso and BPC people became very clear that there were differences between capitalism and socialism. Also they understood the rightful role of Black people in the leadership of our politics. This is a positive position, not jingoism; and it is perfectly discernible in Sactu and the ANC - only last year the ANC allowed a White person for the first time on to its High Command, and we "dare" to say we want what they do. Some of the thinking on this is not as advanced in Lusaka [in the ANC headquarters] as it is amongst us. The traditional approach of the BC movement is seen as being disruptive to the working of UDF and its non-racial Charterist position. I see differences in the two camps. But neither organization fully understands what unity in action could mean. It is very destructive.

> The BC involvement, as I understand it, has become very clear. We seek an anti-racist, socialist society where worker interests are paramount. UDF is talking a lot about an alternative education policy, but they do not have a blueprint for a socialist system. BC has definite ideas, and those equal scientific socialism. It does not have a Black aspect. It has been misinterpreted as a racist con-

cept. This has never been the emphasis. Biko said there is a place for all of us. We are not looking for a Blacks-only Government. There is no way you can conceive of a Black socialist state. What we are emphasizing is that whether you like it or not the indigenous people are Black: it is not racist to say so. There is nothing wrong with the analogy with Britain. The British rule Britain, in the same way Africans should rule South Africa. We want to maintain something which reflects reality. But we are not looking for a "Blacks-only Azania."

In the late 60's, Black Consciousness began to evolve as a philosophy. It used to be very loose - Black is beautiful, Black pride - its first stage. People were losing their identity, we were going to the dogs; the predominant wish was of appearing close to Whites, people were using light skin make up and wigs. So "Black is beautiful" became the response against this and it was important in changing attitudes. In the 70's it was anti-anything that looked like White. It succeeded in stopping the White ideal completely. The second stage: the Black People's Convention projects - health, community projects, sewing. This was to concretize the politicization so it could be seen as real, as responsive to Black people - that Black people can own and administer things - this was about '73/'74. Then 1976 posed new questions. The BC movements were banned. There were liberal inroads into Black politics. A lot of White "democrats" increasingly involved themselves in Black politics. The result - Black on Black confrontation escalating terribly. The first time we find people "necklacing" each other. This time BC applied Marxian analysis-now it was no longer just Black pride. Addressing itself to the situation and adapting a Marxian philosophy to the South African situation, it is conscious of the realities and so interprets it differently from a few years ago. This is different from the loose politics of the ANC's analysis which emphasized the color bar, discrimination in politics and wanted to participate in White politics. In post-'76, BC says we have in South Africa the owners of the means of production and non-owners of means of production; it says further that race divides us into owners and non-owners. Race is a class determinant. It is not by accident that Blacks own no means of production and Whites do have it. '76 was the culmination of BC politicization and mobilization, and unity of Black people. We didn't need to 'necklace' Black people. It was a very exciting unity. Now new organizational conflict has become alarming. Now BC lays emphasis on Marxism. Much as we appreciate Marxism, we do not apply orthodox Marxism because it would confuse our struggle. Therefore we say race is the determination of class. We see a link, a sell-out link,

> between South Africa, America, Britain and a few other countries, as a result of which BC went on to say we are fighting White South Africa, but also capitalism. It is capitalism which has exploited our people and will forever exploit our people. Thus, racial capitalism here exists because of [its support from] American capitalism. Azapo was probably the first to try and isolate South Africa. We have managed to identify the enemy as capitalism - it will annihilate the Black man. We also know that capitalism will try to weaken the conflict between capital and labor through so-called democratic socialism. We are aware of this onslaught: "democracy," "non-racialism," etc., will be sponsored by capitalists. BC says apartheid is a point of departure; the main thing is between capital and labor. So we adopt a Marxian analysis, and we will introduce a Socialist Republic of Azania. And we ask [of ANC and UDF] "Democracy for who?" and we say non-racialism is a loosely interpreted concept. In the French revolution of 1789, people were participating in the revolution on different terms. They came up with vague concepts like fraternity, etc., very loose terms, to suit anybody. So at the end of the Revolution, only the bourgeoisie benefitted.
>
> We must distinguish between political tactics and the ideology of the masses. BC is criticized from a nonracial point of view but BC will remain the hegemonic ideology among the masses of the people as long as racial discrimination remains. BC as a political program may wane but the ideology stays basic to Black people. We want to transfer a Black consciousness to a socialist consciousness. There is more anti-Whiteism in the UDF than in the BC organizations. BC in its old form is on the wane - there is a struggle for the soul of BC among ethnicists and socialists. The more radical elements of BC and the Unity Movement have converged, have grown closer and have formalized this.

It seemed possible, after the state of emergency had taken its toll, that there might be some rethinking on this topic, and that the scale and intensity of Black suffering might lead to a resurgence of Black Consciousness. A few of those interviewed initiated this thought themselves; others were asked about it. BC supporters said they felt that this might be the case. They argued that the repression had forced Black people to see that they had to rely on themselves. It was clear too that there had been too much optimism about the potential impact of the

UDF. People were disappointed and were looking for other answers. Also, it was becoming clear that while Black people were in leadership positions in the UDF, much of the significant research was being done by, and many of the ideas were coming from, White people. This could ultimately undermine the confidence of Black people; that confidence needed to be constantly bolstered and this, in turn, would require a return to BC ideas. Also, it was argued, that the most recent South African elections had forced Black people to a realization that they were on their own. "The liberal pocket of Whites will always move to the side of security when the chips are down." In the same way that White people were returning to their laager to find security, so too, Black people would need to return to theirs. A couple of people suggested that the PAC, which had been ineffective for some time, was also about to make more impact and, while its potential organizational relationship with the BC movement was unclear, it would give a boost to the ideas of the movement.

While these points seem to be cogent, most of the group were convinced that this was not the case. As was noted earlier, the second round of interviews revealed a higher proportion of responses supporting the view that BC was weakening. The increased use by the State of Black vigilantes, informers and Kits Konstabels against Blacks and the continuation of Blacks in the police force continued to challenge a racial analysis of the situation. The ANC commitment to a non-racial future remained constant and continued to be very influential. Also a narrowly racial analysis was as faulty in 1987 as it had been in 1986. Progressive Whites too had suffered in the state of emergency and there was no evidence of these Whites being rejected by Blacks. In other words the majority felt that the events of 1986/87 had not altered the validity of the non-racial analysis and had done nothing to strengthen the hand of the BC movement.

RADICALIZATION CONTINUED

a) RADICALISM CONTINUED: ANTI-CAPITALISM

QUESTION: Do you think that anti-capitalist sentiment is gaining ground among Black South Africans?

Asked - 90; Yes - 64 (71%); No - 12; Conditional - 14; Don't know - 0.

The phenomena of anti-capitalism and support for socialism are clearly closely interlinked. They are not, however, the same: the former may be seen as a reaction against a system, whereas the latter is an alternative to a system; the former may be a necessary prerequisite to the latter or a stage towards the latter; it does not necessarily render it an inevitable outcome. The outcome will depend on time, circumstances, education, and the nature of the struggle, and the changing responses of all the parties, the Government, business, White politicians, Black politicians, the trade unions, and foreign actors both public and private. It is therefore worth distinguishing the two, certainly for purposes of analyzing the dynamics of Black politics.

There was widespread agreement that anti-capitalist sentiment was growing among Black South Africans. There was, however, some disagreement about the depth of feeling; that is, whether people really understood the nature of the system, and whether their hostility was substantive or merely rhetorical and transient; about how widespread it was; that is, whether it was limited to very specific categories of people or was spreading beyond to workers, people in small towns, etc., and as to whether one of its main sources, that is the identification of capitalism with apartheid, was valid or not.

A number of people limited this growing sense of opposition to capitalism to a specific group/category. One view was that this was mainly "the children" again who were getting worked up about this. Others spoke of "Azapo," "certain UDF circles," "trade unions," "trade union leaders," "younger groups," "blue collar workers," "a small section of leaders" and, more inclusively, "sophisticated people, the White left, some Indian and African professionals, UDF leaders and BC leadership." Related to this were serious questions about the depth of feeling. A young Inkatha supporter said that if you spelt out the practicalities of ending capitalism, even to UDF people, they would not really support what they said. "I suspect they don't mean it." And another Inkatha official argued that trade union members did not understand the notion of anti-capitalism. Even some of those interviewees who were more sympathetic to the growth of anti-capitalist feeling acknowledged its limitations. A graduate student agreed that the average Black man would not know the difference, and a trade union organizer said that most workers were simply concerned with improving working conditions. "We will have to teach them," he went on, "about this, and that Black capitalists can oppress them just as much as White capitalists." Other views were that people did not have enough information to be making conscious choices, and that a change of this nature takes time: "the longer the process the more it will evolve." A researcher added:

> It is difficult to know if slogans at a rally are a barometer of real feeling. It is intended to mobilize feelings. And there are plenty of slogans. America represents capitalism, and they are anti-capitalist, and America is the big prop ensuring that the system continues. But deeper down? I don't know.

It must be recorded, however, that most people did not add limitations. These said simply it was increasing. Everyone agreed that to the extent that it was growing, a prime impetus arose from antagonism to the South African Government and its identification with capitalism. It was understood that, increasingly, Black people identified apartheid with capitalism. Whether this identification was valid was not agreed upon, and this is a difference of interpretation which goes to one of the basic divisions in the evolving Black struggle.

A middle aged woman linked to a Cosatu affiliate argued that it was valid:

> Sure. The reason why is because we have made a thorough investigation and worked out that capitalism is the tool of apartheid and the source of oppression and exploitation. The independent trade unions made people aware of this: laymen don't fully understand. But people are very aware that they are being exploited. Salaries are low. White people are sitting in higher positions doing less work and earning more. So we do see capitalism as extracting profits. We see it as rotten.

Another organizer of a union linked to Cosatu agreed:

> For the Black workers, apartheid has been identified with the free market system and it has been severe, brutal and bloody. Therefore, they increasingly question the free market itself. They have got nothing from it for 300 years. It has grossly exploited; it has created inhuman conditions. So we have very big questions about big business running to talk to the ANC without fixing things

> here, and calling for freeing Mandela and unbanning the ANC, and yet not respecting the right to strike and picket here. So workers are increasingly questioning the racist capitalist system.

Nactu-affiliated union organizers made the same points as did students and some of the managerial and UDF people. A banker, who agreed that this was occurring, argued that it was an "erroneous equivalence: anything that is not capitalism has a mystical attraction now." A manager (a strong believer in private enterprise) agreed with the argument that the basis for the hostility was ill-founded:

> People associate it with capitalism and see it as a system which prevents us from participating in free trade and freely offering our labor. On a continuum between a USSR-controlled economy and the USA free market economy, South Africa is far closer to the USSR economy. Capitalists are benefitting from it, but it is not capitalism, it is the opposite.

A private businessman in Port Elizabeth felt that anti-capitalism arose primarily as a reaction against whatever the South African Government favored:

> The funny thing is that if the South African Government says this is "good," we say it is "bad." [Ex-Prime Minister] Vorster was a socialist in the Ossewa Brandwag. P. W. Botha tries to sell us free enterprise. So Blacks regard it with suspicion. That is where it is. Not in a much deeper sense than that. Apartheid and capitalism are not linked. I don't blame them. Generally - people who are oppressed will adopt a system which is an anathema to the regime. Also socialism is inherently attractive to them. We have a race problem. But they see themselves as a proletariat. There is no White proletariat. So they don't need to say Black proletariat.

An Inkatha member working with a foreign corporation in Durban explained:

> It is growing on a small scale partly because America supports it and because Whites are rich. The philosophy of capitalism is not the issue. The issue is that which is being done with it. It is judged as a factor in apartheid. Blacks have suffered from it, and if they know a little about communism, so they will want that alternative. It is not a widespread feeling. To judge capitalism here is

> unfair because we don't have capitalism here: we have socialism in disguise. All the factors of the economy are controlled - licenses to sell, labor, prices - not true capitalism. What if they opened up the economy to Blacks? We would crush Whites. So it is seen as part of the capitalist world and as a western nation, but in reality it is not.

Another issue of significance - although it was raised by only a few people - was that of the receptivity of Blacks to capitalism, socialism or other economic systems. Established Black Consciousness ideology would argue that Blacks were basically and/or traditionally communalistic, and therefore socialistic. This is similar to the case made by Tanzania's Julius Nyerere for African Socialism. Along these lines a community worker claimed that Blacks enjoyed sharing, the responsibility of an extended family, charity and a system of traditional community cooperation. Whites came and called this paganism and tried to destroy it. He did not go on to argue for a return to communalism, but rather that Blacks needed to work out for themselves some fusion of communalism, socialism and capitalism. An elderly man, senior in the UDF, agreed:

> Albert Luthuli [past President of the ANC and a Nobel Peace Prize winner] used to say that our model was the Labor Party in Britain. It would be very easy to introduce it. Our use of land, for example is communal. Our rights, our defence, our means of production, are all controlled by the tribe. There is individual ownership of livestock and land is cultivated for your own benefit. So it is nothing new for us to think of the increase in production as being communally owned. A company is also run by a group of people, not an individual. So a tribe - which is like a system of shareholders - and a company are similar. Private ownership is recognized at the same time as there is communal ownership. This is not strange to us.

By contrast, a woman academic observed that "our people are immersed in capitalist values. Cars, houses, dresses, dressing their children. Conspicuous consumption has caught us. Marxism will not take. So there is no need to worry about it."

A man whose task it was to counsel Black businessmen asserted that everybody had the urge to become an entrepreneur and to eventually own a company; that is, they were capitalists in the true sense. "This is not an anti-capitalist society. Only activists are interested in anti-capitalism; and they are not getting through to the people." A third view, that of a student, was that anti-capitalist or pro-capitalist dispositions depended in the final analysis not on African tradition or culture but on one's class situation: "where he is at the time. As soon as I participate in capitalism I won't attack it. If I don't participate I will be anti-capitalist." He felt that the mushrooming of divisions and splits in the Black movement resulted from this. He also said that Black leaders were all taking off for the elite areas of the townships. Only one person, a businessman, raised the issue of ANC policy as a possible determining influence: in his view the organization had not worked out an economic policy and therefore the topic was still up for discussion. He did, however, go on to warn that corporations that did not allow Black businessmen to participate in both ownership and decision-making were likely to be nationalized one day.

It is very clear from this discussion that the prime reason for the growing anti-capitalism was the suffering of Black people under a system known to them as capitalist or free enterprise, and almost all the responses dealt with this question. A trade unionist saw the connection between capitalism and racism in terms that went beyond the particulars of the South African situation:

> Yes, we identify capitalism with oppression. Capitalism internationally, especially in the third world, feeds on racism. Here it takes the form of apartheid; but even in the Orient people feel that the ownership of most major companies is still foreign and there is a contradiction between the third world and capitalism. In the words of Basil Davidson the experience of the third world is that imperialism and capitalism feed on racism.

America's role in South Africa as a cause of anti-capitalism was mentioned here by only a small number of the group. A journalist, noted that the debate over sanctions helped to crystalize the Black opposition to capitalism. People were anti-capitalist because they were victims of capitalism and America was "the Ayatollah of capitalism." An Inkatha businessman and a UDF academic made very similar comments about America being seen to support White people and rich people, and since it was itself capitalist this had created a negative image. (Britain and West Germany were also mentioned.) An Azapo supporter saw a clear link between anti-capitalism and hostility to American imperialism. For him these feelings arose from issues far beyond South Africa. He mentioned as examples the American bombing of Libya (which we will return to), and support for Unita in Angola (an issue of great emotional significance which he said almost led to Unita delegates being killed when they visited Witwatersrand University). The anger caused by these policies, and the demonstrations against Edward Kennedy, demonstrated that people were analyzing the US as an imperialist power. He also spoke of songs that were sung about this, how Azasm and Black Consciousness groups would be the first to bring socialism to South Africa, and attacking America, colonialism and imperialism.

Another person noted that in contrast to capitalist interests which opposed sanctions, "people who are 100% opposed to the oppression of Blacks are from socialist states" and this added to the anti-capitalist feeling. While noting that these points were made, it is of interest that so few people made mention of the American-capitalism connection in responding to this question.

Finally, note should be taken of the dynamics of intra-Black politics as a source of anti-capitalism. One person mentioned that Buthelezi and Inkatha were forcing unions and workers to choose between Cosatu and Uwusa and between socialism and capitalism. The trade unions, he said, did not want to move too fast on this subject, but there was now an open challenge, and this was likely to hasten the move to a more clearly anti-capitalist posture. He added that there was growing suspicion of US support for Buthelezi which would intensify the hostility.

Buthelezi's support for capitalism will be relevant to perceptions of capitalism and make it more difficult for pro-free enterprise opponents of Buthelezi to defend capitalism. A further aspect is that there does appear to be a race on to capture the "extreme left" of the movement. A UDF supporter accused BC people of trying to corrupt the left side of the struggle in going further than the left of the UDF in its anti-capitalist posturing. In the heat of the struggle, and in face of tremendous suffering, extremism is more likely to suit the emotional needs of those effected. The stronger the attack the more appropriate it will seem. A number of people mentioned this phenomenon as being visible at public meetings and funerals.

b) RADICALISM CONTINUED: SOCIALISM

QUESTION: In your opinion, is socialism growing among Black South Africans?

Asked - 91; Yes - 60 (66%); No - 12; Conditional - 18; Don't know - 1.

A few of the interviewees who sensed a growing anti-capitalist sentiment were not prepared to conclude that socialism, as a clear alternative, was on the increase. Their view was that the acceptance of socialist ideals was too superficial and rhetorical to be taken seriously. A number of people who said it was increasing made similar points. While the overall response shows a clear majority in agreement that it was growing, the clarity and conviction and fullness of its acceptance was in general seen to be somewhat weaker than the anti-capitalism discussed above.

People in the group offered reasons for socialism gaining ground. These overlap with those mentioned in explaining increased anti-capitalism. It was generated by the huge scale of poverty, unemployment and lack of opportunity and hope among Blacks, particularly among the youth. "We are angry with the present monster. If this monster is such a murderer, let us give the other a try." Capitalism was badly represented by the Government which was obviously excluded from presenting its own case at political rallies where socialism was gaining a lot of rhetorical support. Socialist countries have continued to give material help and have shown consistent understanding of the Black struggle. The victories of the radically socialist-oriented liberation forces in Mozambique, Angola and Zimbabwe had a strong impact on the direction of the struggle. People were looking for a society in which the ideals were peace, participation and equality and where there would be no small, rich, dominant minority. Finally, a person who was thinking less about the humanitarian ideals and more about the non-democratic elements of some socialist systems put further blame on the Botha Government and specifically the most recent state of emergency:

> Young people are thinking of communism proper. For example they call each other "comrade". They are going for power which is concentrated so that they will be in a position to get things done. There is a tendency for groups to listen to one person. It is not very easy to remain democratic. We have been deprived of our platforms - if these were still available there would still be democratic discussion and decisions. For example, Graca [Grahamstown Civic Association] was a popular organization for the people. It got into difficulty with its leaders being arrested and now a small group must decide for the community. It is the Government which pushes the young people to be communist - especially the state of emergency. The street committees were democratic. It is very difficult now because a wide range of decisions need to be made.

This topic will be dealt with by moving from those who said that socialism was not increasing, to those who said a "limited yes," to those who gave clear answers to the effect that it was growing.

An elderly technical assistant, opposed to socialism, said that "nobody" - and that included the youth - was becoming socialist. People simply wanted to improve their positions and win political participation; they did not want dominance. A graduate, a supporter of the ANC, also denied it was increasing (and he was critical that this was the case). The average person simply wanted to "live luxuriously ... they don't want to share. They want to live like you." Even the trade unions, he felt, were capitalizing on management mistakes to motivate workers and were not really trying to educate them toward socialism. "I've seen them strike for money; they are not politically conscious." And a shop steward said:

> We are just wanting to teach workers about management tricks and just want workers to know about their rights and procedures, disciplinary procedures, etc. What workers must do, how to use committees. Also about profits ... try to explain the hierarchy of the establishment and who gets the profits. We want some control for workers. They are angry about profits and that they don't receive living wages. The unions did get them to improve wages.

According to a middle aged woman executive working in Johannesburg:

> The children talk about it a lot, but they are not clear what they mean. When pushed on this they talk about communalism and using it in a modern setting. We have no contact, concern, empathy with the Soviet Union and Eastern Europe, and this goes also for workers and students. So capitalism and apartheid are seen as close, but we are not clear about socialism. But we must control the economy, not like African states. All South Africa's neighbors are vulnerable because they don't control their economies.

A young woman, a community organizer in the Eastern Cape, said:

> We are not sure about the alternative program. The South Africa Communist Party wanted socialism, but this was not on. We need social democracy and this is what the Freedom Charter stands for. It implies the need to control big business, but not to get rid of it.

An executive working for a private foundation in Soweto said:

> People are confused. Socialism might work for us Blacks. People are talking about a new model which we can't define. We need to be able to compete freely at the market place. The unions are not clear. But it does make sense, to unions. But it has failed elsewhere. Students are confused and most of us are confused. We want everybody equal, and equality of opportunity. I believe Blacks are capitalist in tendency. Everything will have a tinge of capitalism whatever the mode.

A woman academic research officer stated:

> People do have a desire for it. But when they face up to it squarely, they have doubts. Students liked Nyerere's Ujamaa till they heard about the low salaries [in Tanzania] - they are young capitalists. This is the course of intellectualism - debating endlessly about things they don't believe in.

An academic councillor in Natal explained:

> It is the alternative to the evil they experience, not an analysis of what they will do. The devil you don't know is an angel as long as you are faced with the present one. I don't think we would kick and scream if the transfer of power came and it wasn't socialist.

An Inkatha urban representative argued:

> The leadership of some organizations is becoming more socialist. But they are isolated in this. We do hear more from the trade unions about socialism. The youth are spread all over - some are pro- and some anti-capitalist. The majority are anti-capitalist. The masses have no time to discuss these things.

A senior trade union organizer interjected two further points of relevance here. One was that capitalism was not remaining passive and this could be seen in the new offers of shares to Black employees and some encouragement being given to Black capital - "in its limited and inexperienced form" - to buy into shopping plazas and bus companies. The second was to keep in mind the distinction between belief in socialism, which he judged to be on the increase, and practice; it was obviously problematic to operate in a socialist manner in South Africa at present, but to the extent that it was possible he saw few signs of commitment to practice.

A second category of responses came from those in the group who felt it was gaining in a somewhat more significant way, but was still at an early stage in its development. A young researcher argued that it was at an immature stage, at least partly because debate had for so long been restricted by the State. People used to be too scared. This had changed now. Discussion was more open and Blacks were gaining confidence. The trade unions for example were using the terminology of socialism more freely. He was concerned however that some of what he referred to as "ideologues in the UDF" wanted to follow Lenin's model - "We question whether the Soviet Union has really been liberated" - and this worried socialists who wanted a national democracy; and also that South African socialist theoreticians were being treated like gods. A graduate student, a supporter of the ANC, in his mid 20's, analyzed the situation in the following way:

> More people are seeing it as a solution, though the level of understanding may be low. Trade unions, aren't sure- they are still mainly concerned with bread and butter issues. So young people are pushing it. UDF are not socialist. They are still trying to translate feelings of everyone who wants to share. They are democratic rather than having any clear direction. They want equal pay, equal voting rights, equality in personal life, and realize the need for some control of the economy, but they are not clear.

A final year Azapo student said:

> It is growing. Generally most Black people don't comprehend the full implications. People have not reached a commitment beyond return. It could swing back to capitalism. It is growing mainly among workers. Also Black culture is generally favorable toward socialism. People in rural areas share - unlike White society. Traditional society is important to us. We are uncomfortable with too much individualism. The principles of Azapo are designed to ensure that the struggle is not hijacked by opportunists. It is anti-imperialist, anti-collaborationist and anti-racist. It is more socialist than the UDF. Azapo type of socialism is not a social welfare state. We criticize UDF and the Freedom Charter as advocating social welfare. We believe that you must change the economic power relations, workers must control the means of production and own the means of production. Worker interests must be uppermost.

A journalist responded:

> They are strongest on what they don't want. But on what they do want they are unsure. What we know about socialism is in theory; we have no experience in practice. We support anything the Government does not want. We

> observed a moment's silence for Brezhnev's death - to show our opposition to the South African Government.

A young Cosatu-affiliated trade unionist, himself a socialist, said:

> It is increasing, but it is very small. One thing is that the leadership is talking about it. The majority of people don't have a clear understanding. Of late, trade unions have been overwhelmed by people joining. This is the effect of capitalism at the work place, the hardships in the townships, and increasingly people see the link between capitalism and apartheid. At our training sessions these issues are being discussed. Also in political and community organizations.

A BC trade union organizer stated:

> We are turning to alternatives to capitalism. But we are not clear about what alternatives we want. In [our] unions we discuss various options - welfare states (e.g., Scandinavian states), the role of the party, of unions? We are very concerned about the trade union movement being free and democratic and not being dictated to by the party. We want to insure a free and independent trade union movement with its own integrity. The last thing we want is to unseat apartheid and find a one-party system with no freedom for trade unions.

A middle-aged priest agreed:

> Africans are becoming more socialist. We hear more and more about socialism from young people. They have become strongly anti-capitalist. This is not because of what they know of the African [continent's] experience, but because of their own experience. For example, here in ..., the extremes of poverty and wealth are so big that they want a system which will distribute benefits better, so that those who have more than enough will surrender something to those who need. Young people don't read like we used to and less literature is available. Kids dream of a socialist economy where the people will control capitalists etc. This is not realistic. Adults will prevail. We will get them to see this is not realistic.

Moving on to a third type of answer to this question on socialism, there were those who were more convinced that it was growing noticeably. For example, a business executive - a strong proponent of the free enterprise system - saw it growing in the unions. In his view, unions accepted the profit motive but disliked the stock market mechanism, speculation and huge wealth, the fact that Whites controlled access to capital, while the bulk of work was carried out by Black workers. Since they did not get a fair share of the return, they were rebelling against the shareholders. "They want worker control of the factories, to be on the board, and to be the shareholders. They would take over foreign companies, or allow them a minority share." While he did not think that most workers were familiar with socialism, he did feel that the leadership, which was educated, outspoken and articulate, did have a socialist political agenda. A middle-level manager with a private foundation (an ex-union official) saw it increasing because of Soviet help. While it might still be a fashion, it could turn out to be dangerous. "During funerals, the red flag is flying. Youngsters are wearing socialist attire. It is coming and it definitely relates to anti-Americanism." Another manager, also with a union background, explained:

> People are tired of rule by the National Party, and the Progressive Party seems to be going in the same direction. Hence, leaders are coming up with socialism as an answer to our aspirations. Leaders of Cosatu unions are conscientizing illiterate workers to want to own and control their enterprises; they want to go further than just participating in decisions. The youth too. Here also the leaders are conscientizing the masses. Moderates and the middle class are worried about this; they are afraid. The kids tell the parents to stop their children from going to school. Parents argue. Kids shout them down. In the meetings of Payco and Pepco, etc., students are involved. Young boys address the meetings and people accept. Even at union meetings, kids talk. They push socialism hard.

A BC supporter, a graduate researcher in his 30's, answered:

> Yes. A kind of humanitarian socialism, like Kaunda. It would be aimed at sharing. Not really communism. But socialism is growing. BC looks to Africa for lessons. The

> ANC looks to the Soviet Union. We look more to the Chinese than to the Russians.

A banker commented:

> There is an examination of which social system they want; this is not just rhetoric. It worries me in particular. People who used to endorse the free enterprise system now do not.

A Cosatu-affiliated union organizer in his late twenties said:

> What it would look like is still open. But there is a general drift to socialism. One can question how it is seen by different independent trade union movements. We have accepted the following principles: 1) worker control of the factory and the community; 2) non-racialism; 3) regular reporting, mandated and full accountability; and 4) democracy and an open society. These elements are central to the trade union movement.

A woman connected with a Cosatu-related union stated:

> It is taken quite seriously. The people are looking for it and aiming at it if liberation comes. It is still in a discussion stage in the movement. The first thing is to press management to involve workers in all the structures of all the companies - this is something which is still very difficult. The workers are aiming at taking over the companies - they produce, and therefore they should control resources as they produce them. These are very strong issues in discussion with workers.

Moving on to more clearly affirmative statements about the growth of socialism, an Azapo supporter working with a church -sponsored organization said that in many of their songs they sang about socialism and of the claim that they would bring it to South Africa before others. A young community organizer who would support the ANC said:

> We see better what we are fighting. We know that it is not about government only. We know that we must take over the economic structures as well. We are talking more and more seriously about socialism; and looking at Russia and Cuba as models. We used to be pro-US; then we became just as simply pro-Soviet. Now we are talking seriously about experiences and policies. We are seriously committed to this, and we have gone a long way beyond

> communalism. Workers too have become far more conscious of this. Anti-capitalism is very strong. The workers are increasingly pro-socialist. They talk about taking over factories, running them, protecting them against attacks from the right. This is based on experience here and the view of capitalism here. We now know that money from foreign corporations doesn't stay here - it goes out of the country. Younger people are far less religious than older people, and religious leader's concerns about socialism are not held by younger people.

A UDF office holder in Natal, who was himself strongly pro-socialist, agreed:

> It is growing at an increasing rate. It is a serious alternative and it is almost inevitable. Steps will be discussed but the objective is communism. Barayi has been thrown in as a leader of Cosatu. But he is out of step [this refers to a statement by the Cosatu president accepting the model of the British Labor Party]. It will happen in two stages. Young people and workers are in favor of communism. Older and professional people and some workers are in favor of social democracy. The former will inevitably win.

Another UDF office-holder, in the Transvaal, also saw a process of increasing acceptance of socialism under way. He pointed to a less dramatic but probably more widespread trend. In a carefully explained and important statement he pointed to the changing interpretation of the Freedom Charter.

> There is no doubt that such a process is under way. Example one: all shall participate in the running of the country. This is open to different interpretations. It may mean participating in the existing Parliament; another is the convening of a constituent assembly to work out ways of governing the country. The trend is increasingly to move away from the existing Parliament to a constituent assembly of all organizations being represented. Here you have the beginnings of the idea of soviets and constituencies. There is clearly a shift to the left and the longer the struggle the more this will occur. Example two: in the Freedom Charter it says wealth shall be more fairly shared. Interpretations range from fairer wages for all to fairer distribution of all facilities to the other extreme of redistribution of capital and the country. Here the same trend is taking place. Both ideas existed in the old Democratic Movement, but the trend now is towards the latter view, because the problems in South Africa are not being solved.

> Example three: ownership of land. There are two ideas about its meaning; that peasants and landless people be given some land and that the purchase of the land and resettlement of people be done by the State. The other view sees the seizure of all land and its redistribution to and by the people. The movement again is clearly towards the seizure and redistribution of the land, rather than the first. Example four: education. People used to think of equal distribution of resources between population groups, that is, an opening of doors of learning and culture to all. But now the move is towards a wholesale reorganization of education to reflect norms and values of an oppressed people. We hear of "People's Education" and "Education for liberation." One sees the emergence of street committees rudimentary organizations of people's power, the beginnings of a new administration for land, education, capital, and so on.

The same speaker then returned to the long-standing dilemma of whether to place priority on national liberation or socialism.

> Clearly, anti-capitalism and socialism are growing in the country, although people see national liberation as a crucial problem. If one is going to have a consensus of as broad a spectrum of people as possible, then national liberation is fundamental. That is the first objective. In striving for that objective, however, radicalization is taking place. Those who favor a socialist solution eventually publicly espouse national liberation. Some people only want to be part of a ruling group. Others acknowledge national liberation as a first step, as a minimum consensus to unite us. But we must, in the meanwhile, educate people to solve our fundamental problems of land, capital and education. Very few people would advocate a socialist program. Yet most would stress national liberation first coupled with a long term goal of socialism. Workerists are concerned that if there is no fundamental change now, we won't have a socialist answer ever, and they will be betrayed. We say there is no chance of being betrayed. There is no doubt of the shift to the left over time. The longer the process the more it will take place. I see this clearly over time.

c) RADICALISM CONTINUED: AFFECTS ON PERCEPTIONS OF THE UNITED STATES

The nexus between radicalism on the one hand and hostility toward the US is a key component of this Study. To return to the notions mentioned in the Introduction; a possible continuum is being investigated. The longer the revolution continues, the more radical it becomes; the more radical it becomes, the more anti-capitalist and pro-socialist it will be; and the more anti-capitalist and pro-socialist it becomes the more hostile towards the United States it will get. Asking about the connection between radicalism and changing attitudes to America is therefore a central question.

However, while it is a question that therefore had to be asked, it was also a question that it would have been better not to need to ask. It would have been better in the sense of being more convincing if the answers had emerged spontaneously in response to other questions. There is a further problem here. It relates to the attempt to distinguish a relatively superficial antagonism to President Reagan and the policy of Constructive Engagement from a deeper more long term radicalism. For there can be no doubt that, even without the latter, anger would have grown. Yet one also needs to keep in mind that President Reagan's policies and the way they are perceived are themselves playing a significant part in radicalizing Black South Africans. This will be returned to in the Conclusion.

QUESTION: Do you think that this growing anti-capitalism and pro-socialism is having an impact on attitudes to the US?

Asked - 71; Yes - 48 (73% of those who gave an answer); No - 15; Conditional - 3; Don't know - 5.

Keeping these issues in mind it is nevertheless clear that, having asked the question, the majority of responses were firmly positive that there was a definite spillover from internal attitudes onto perceptions of America.

The few who felt that the connection was slim argued that the radicalism remained "about local events, local laws and the privileges of Whites - it is only in Azapo circles that people see the US as imperialist" - and that most people did not understand America's involvement, "nor do they care: they see Pretoria as the enemy."

A couple of people who did not deny the connection put the pieces together in slightly different ways. A student adviser at one of the universities said: "To the extent that America is seen as supporting Botha, America is affected. But capitalism is incidental to the issue. Capitalism suffers because the US is associated with the South African Government; it is not that the US Government suffers because it is capitalist." Someone else added: "If the people are against capitalism then America will see them as in favor of communism. And so we get angry with them."

The following are some of the ways in which people explained how they saw the relationship. To begin with, a middle-aged woman, working for a voluntary organization, analyzed the connection in this way.

> Because we know for sure that America's sole purpose is profit. They don't care who makes it and how it is made. They only want a profit. That is why we feel they should get out or allow us to share. We play a very important role in their products and we need to share in their profits. Imperialism is talked of a lot at public meetings. Also it comes up in labor education which makes this clear.

A businessman, in his forties, said:

> America has become the enemy. It is also tied to the American attitude to the ANC. They never talk to the ANC properly. America is seen by the world-wide revolutionary movement as a stumbling block to revolutionary governments throughout the world. We see America as the capitalist policeman of the world.

A senior executive in a private company added:

> America will have do to something relevant and dramatic. We don't talk about imperialism. But we do see America as the champion of capitalism. At a political rally organized by Cosatu or at funerals, that is where the South African Government will be attacked and mention will be made of the USA helping the South African Government because of capitalist interests. At mass meetings we keep hearing these things. The atmosphere is emotional in all cases. Regularly, speaker after speaker attacks America. America needs to portray a better side of capitalism. South Africa has abused the free enterprise system.

A UDF organizer in Natal stated:

> America is the bastion of western capitalism. It has never been in the forefront of the struggle of a working class. Never. In Angola it opposes, in Nicaragua, in Cuba it opposes socialist regimes.

A young university lecturer made the same point that America had come to represent capitalism, accumulation and profit and that its record in Cuba, Nicaragua and Angola proved that it stood for exploitation above all else. It was clear that the US was under suspicion for taking money out of the country in the form of profits and for bringing it back in the form of aid. An educationist in Cape Town referred to a virtual invasion of South Africa by US money and the fear this caused that Blacks may find themselves trapped in a US conspiracy to control their future. A manager, working for a foundation which disbursed US money, confirmed that some Black organizations that badly needed assistance refused to take US aid. They feared it would be used by the Reagan Administration as propaganda to show that the US was supporting authentic Black organizations. "So they would rather suffer." It must also be noted that a good number of Black organizations were accepting US financial support.

A first-year student, a UDF supporter, said that the assistance and support that came to the ANC from the East was helping to "estrange" people from capitalism and the US: the future of this process would depend on which side would help liberate Blacks. A first year student (a BC supporter) commented:

> Yes. Only to a small extent for the man in the street. Definitely for the leadership because we experience such problems with American corporations. People do talk a lot about imperialism. For example, the raid on Libya - we hero worship Qaddafi: because we saw the raid as aggressive and imperialist. The term gets used a lot, especially in BC groups. Angola is also a good example. Unita is seen as an imperialist force and Savimbi as a lackey. So assistance to Unita from the US highlights US imperialism.

A middle-aged academic said:

> Clearly. If ownership of the means of production is important to our struggle, and if the US is seen as the bastion of capitalism and wants to retain a particular system. Probably all along there has been some antagonism to the US, but it is strengthening at the grass roots level. The more politically educated conscious people saw the camp that American capital is trying to organize. Now the rank and file is seeing it more clearly. Change is wanted and America is against it.

The notion that America was trying to organize "a camp" to retain capitalism cropped up in various places in the interviews - this may have refered to Inkatha, or businessmen and their organizations and middle class Blacks. There was considerable concern about this. Finally a journalist commented:

> Certainly it does. Black people today find it more and more difficult to see a difference between apartheid and capitalism. If America is seen as the Ayatollah of capitalism, America will be seen as insincere when it condemns apartheid because it amounts to condemning itself.

Four threads of radicalism have been investigated: violence, Black Consciousness, anti-capitalism and socialism. An acceptance that some violence is necessary to pressure White people to accept change and a readiness to engage in acts of violence have both grown. This, it was pointed out repeatedly, was not the choice of Black people, but the only avenue of expression Pretoria had left available to them. The influence of Black Consciousness, as espoused in the late sixties and seventies seems to have weakened considerably. ANC-UDF non-racialism appeared to be dominant, and the BC movement has evolved away from its earlier preoccupations, taking on a more socialist orientation.

There seems no doubt that anti-capitalism has grown quite dramatically from say 15 years earlier and that people were increasingly coming to oppose it as well as apartheid, and to see that both political and economic structures were involved in their oppression. Black people, and all would agree, know that they are being economically exploited. Clearly, too, this sense of growing hostility was most clearly understood and articulated at the leadership level; but at that level it has spread across large elements of UDF, trade unions, youth organizations, BC organizations, and certainly religious leaders have also publicly acknowledged the injustice of capitalism. What was also clear was that it was spreading. As the economy deteriorated, as the leaders educated their followers, as there was increasing use of strikes, consumer boycotts, stay-aways, calls for sanctions, all of which pitted Blacks against capitalist institutions, the level of antagonism was rising. Socialism was also being seen in a more positive light, particularly at a leadership level, and various models were being investigated for their possible appropriate application to a post-apartheid society. Trade unions and youth organizations were probably most advanced in this regard. In both cases, leaders were actively interested in educating their followers. There was also some fairly strong evidence that these trends in the radicalization of Black South Africans, at however early a stage they may still have been, were, together with other influences (which were interrelated), such as President Reagan's speeches and actions, influencing Black perceptions of America and its future role in South Africa.

U.S. CORPORATIONS, THE CIVIL RIGHTS MOVEMENT AND PERCEPTIONS OF THE U.S.

a) US CORPORATIONS

So far, the main area of focus has been on official US policy towards South Africa, and the response of Black South Africans to that policy. In South Africa, as in most other countries of the world, attitudes toward the US will be determined not only by American Government policy, but also by the behavior of US corporations; and in this case most specifically by the way they relate to Black employees and the cause of Black liberation. Far more Blacks have had and continue to have direct connections with a US company than with the US Government. It must be recalled too that for most of the time that US companies have operated in the country they have taken advantage of the apartheid system to employ Black labor at very low wages; and this went unquestioned by management. It is only more recently that the performance of American business has come under close scrutiny both in the US and in South Africa. Their manner of operation has an important bearing on the way in which Black South Africans view the US.

QUESTION: What is your assessment of the behavior of US corporations in South Africa? Positive or negative?

Asked - 77; Negative - 49 (64%); Positive - 14; Conditional- 14; Don't know - 0.

QUESTION: Do you think that there is any possibility that they may yet play a positive role in the liberation of Black South Africans?

Asked - 66; No - 32 (48%); Yes - 29; Conditional - 5: Don't know - 0.

The two questions were coupled: one asked what their general assessment was of US corporate behavior and the second asked whether they thought there was any possibility at all of these companies playing a constructive role in their liberation. The breadth of the second part ("that there is any possibility" rather than "it is likely") was stressed to allow interviewees to include the possibility of changing corporate behavior in their responses. Most discussion centered on the first question. In this regard some of the group made mention of the Sullivan Principles and used them as a sort of vague measuring stick against which to test standards of corporate behavior. These principles have also given focus to those in the US concerned with watching the performance of these enterprises. Matters such as salaries, benefits, training, promotions, housing, recreation facilities and integration of staff generally were covered. In addition, the firms' willingness to deal with trade unions and to provide extra-mural (political) support for the cause of Black freedom were included.

As most Black leaders have become more assertive and more convinced that disinvestment and sanctions were essential to freedom, so Black political appeals to the corporate community have become more demanding and, for businessmen, sometimes confusing. As will be seen, their Black critics pointed to a variety of concerns, from low salaries to resistance to disinvestment to failure to break the law as a way of forcing the Government to alter course. Different respondents were looking at different aspects of corporate performance. Overall, however, the large majority of those who gave a definite answer one way or another held a negative view of the performance of these companies.

To begin with, the views of the minority who saw these firms in a positive light will be dealt with. A technical assistant who did not work for a US firm but ran a community project in a township with money from the US had this to say:

> I am very positive about US corporations. They pay equal wages. They treat people much better than South African companies. They do good services. I am involved in working with US money on community projects. They can be constructively involved in the change, and I would very much like them to be.

A second person who was positive was a shop steward in a major union affiliated to Cosatu who had lost his job earlier for leading a major strike against his employers. His credentials as a concerned and responsive union official could not be questioned.

> American companies must not leave because that will increase unemployment. They should try to organize themselves in South Africa and maybe the big bosses of the American companies can come together to solve the problem and send representatives to the Government. If they withdraw, that will cause a lot of trouble. Even if apartheid is solved because the companies go away, it will be too expensive for them to come back. South African companies and American companies are different, because

> American companies can pay a little bit of a living wage and South African companies do not.

A third positive comment came from a woman serving on the faculty of a university. While she was very critical of US policies, she saw the companies as making a useful contribution.

> Corporations have created a demand for skills. They have broken down barriers. Children used to aim to be teachers, policemen. Today we talk of engineers - all because of industrialization. They could do more. They could help to bring liberation by moving into Black education, informal and formal, into community, and self help....

Inkatha supporters expressed gratitude for the jobs they created as well as for their donations to local projects and the scholarships they offered. One official said:

> I am positive. They have not gone full out but the little they do is positive. Their utterances, their small financial aid is effective. They could do more. The corporations can't do anything on their own. But they should be part and parcel of convincing the South African Government. In their home countries they should spread the gospel of change. They must invest as much as possible to facilitate job creation.

Positive assessments were, however, in the minority. A few others gave mixed responses. An executive in his thirties, trained in the US, possibly the most pro-US non-Inkatha person in the group, noted that they had dome some positive things but that they needed to get their act together because their Black advancement programs "generally stink." A businessman felt that some of them had good intentions, but the "people running them are no good." When the policies of the company meet the "middle level right-wing bureaucrat" they are negated by "destructive obstructionists." This point about the policy-intention of the foreign company being good, but the implementation, as executed by White middle to senior level South Africans, being poor (the so-called "internal company culture") was made by a few people. A young research officer in Natal acknowledged that they now paid higher wages and provided a better working environment than locally based firms. While they had therefore gone beyond the "slave driver mentality" their profit motive still led them to use the apartheid structures to their advantage and to keep quiet about it. As a result of certain "prompts" like the Sullivan Code, the events of 1976, threats of consumer boycotts and pressure for sanctions, they had made quite a number of improvements. "They are changing jockeys but they are still running the same horse in the races."

The next three quotations illustrate the differing nature of the expectations and of the criticisms of US companies. First, an executive's view:

> Their image is changing slightly. Some can be singled out for positive things, for example, dealing with the trade unions and treating their people well. General Motors lately received good comments because its manager offered to pay the fines of his Black workers who might be prosecuted for swimming on Whites-only beaches [in Port Elizabeth]. The way Ford left here left a bad impression. It took a profit for a long time and then it suddenly pulled out leaving thousands jobless. American companies could be constructive; but the [Black] people they train in the US come back and are treated as juniors in front of the workers. This alienated the workers and the trainees. Here in the Eastern Cape, Ford has become America.

A Port Elizabeth businessman's view:

> People must not lose sight of the fact that pulling out is to force the South African Government to the negotiating table. This is the only way to avoid violence. People are willing to suffer. Their presence is not helping to bring about change. As long as you are comfortable you won't negotiate. Corporations have assisted Blacks in many ways. But they should get out.

A Witwatersrand University graduate student's opinion:

> Some more liberal corporations grant certain concessions to Black workers and, for example, give them off on May Day

> and June 16th. They are not as staunch as national and other foreign companies. But as capitalists they do that in their own interest. It bolsters their ability to suck profits with an easier image and their workers don't become so militant and openly challenging.

Moving on to those, the majority, who were unconditionally critical, the main distinction was between those who felt there was a chance still, not a big one, but a possibility, of US companies playing some constructive role in helping Black people to reach their freedom, and those who had concluded that this was no longer possible. Clearly, policy consequences will arise from such a distinction. For the first group, a marked and immediate change in the role of US companies would mean that they would be welcome to stay. But the view of the latter, the assumption being that this was impossible, was that the companies should go, and the sooner the better. Given the radicalism and the anti-capitalism discussed in the previous chapter, one would have expected this attack (which was very strong) to have been more clearly related to an analysis of the expected behavior of international capitalist enterprises. In fact, the criticism was overwhelmingly based on their reading of the empirical evidence. As a senior executive with a private foundation in Johannesburg said:

> US business has a poor record, but definitely there is hope. They must do something to ensure the free enterprise system and they must deliver soon. We can relate US business to the Black community concerns in order to bring about peaceful change. I am a moderate. If I did not believe this I would not be here. We must keep foreign companies and use them. They will use us, and we must be prepared to be used in order to use them.

Another executive, also with a private foundation said:

> American companies all took advantage of apartheid to make a profit. Some more; some less. Sullivan [Code] was phony. The monitoring was phony, and none of the companies responded to the fourth principle of extra-business support for Blacks. I can't really think of one company that was really good before the current pressure. General-

> ly, there is great cynicism about recent changes. We need to keep American companies. Disinvestment is a temporary request. So, after the change, they can return as friends of ours. If they stay now, we will tell them to get out and not come back.

As pointed out above, a number of those who said they could play a useful role stressed that they thought this was very unlikely. A technical assistant in his late thirties explained:

> They have not adhered to the Sullivan Principles. This is just idle talk in the press. They don't live up to what they say. Some are very pro-apartheid. The American Government shouldn't allow this but it does. They could help. If they lived up to the Sullivan Code, the anti-Americanism would subside because it would mean that America was living up to its word. I don't know if it could happen. It's like throwing a dice.

A first year student, a UDF supporter, was even less hopeful:

> They didn't use to care. Now because of the violence their future is endangered. So now they are trying to ameliorate their position with the Black people. ... They could play a role. But I despair.

And last among those who were strongly critical but felt there was still hope, a banker, strongly in favor of private enterprise, commented:

> They could play a constructive role but they have failed dismally. They have failed to get their houses in order and so have perpetuated things in South Africa. They have held back on programs inside their corporations in South Africa which would have won them Black allies. They have good policies at the top. But they have been dragged back by the traditional way of life in South Africa, and so failed to implement because of the White core of middle management.

Finally, in dealing with views on US corporations in the country, we turn to those who had concluded that there was no helpful role for these firms. Firstly, in the view of a priest, the American Government had made very cynical use of the Sullivan Principles, making no effort whatever to enforce them. "I can't see how we could possibly involve US companies in the struggle for liberation. I can't see how." A young community organizer in Grahamstown, strongly opposed to America's position in South Africa, had this to say:

> We are aware that there are some with decent concerns; for example those that signed the Sullivan Principles. We know that they give scholarships and have paid better wages. But generally the image is very negative. They profit here. They help support the Government. If they give things to Blacks they also will sponsor - and this is very big now - White sports and cultural events. And this is our money. Even the better companies anger us with this. Really, it is too late. They will improve conditions and wages, and negotiate. But the workers will demand more and more. They are five years too late. Also they will not put pressure on the South African Government.

A middle level manager employed in the private sector was even harsher:

> They stink. They are here for the money. They rip off whatever they can and go. Look at the people who come here from the States. They are arrogant. They don't improve the situation. They had to be forced to do token things to earn "Brownie points." They can't be of any use in liberating us. Take IBM. Blacks who work there carry a title, but no power. They are looked down upon as inefficient, lazy, etc. They deliberately chose people who would be submissive, humble, weak and were sure to fail.

An experienced UDF supporter made the sort of criticism that indicates how complex the predicament of foreign companies has become and how in the eyes of some influential Blacks they can no longer do any good:

> American companies use some of their profit for winning the support of inhabitants of this country. In doing this they help the State by paying for scholarships, clinics. The State should be providing these. So they substitute for the State and let the State off what it should be doing. So it is easier for the State to buy and pay for instruments of oppression, soldiers and weapons.

A young legal services adviser added:

> The sooner they pack up the better. They aren't doing any good. They can't be of use to the struggle. They are planting poison in the liberation movement. They are playing the same games here that they are playing in Zimbabwe.

A first year student, a BC supporter, commented:

> It depends on what freedom you are talking about. If it is only a non-racial society, they could be of some help. Obviously they can't help with a socialist liberation.

Finally, a Soweto journalist concluded:

> They are not helpful. If these corporations have good jobs and good pay, this affects a very small part of what the struggle is about. This is not a struggle about civil rights, but about power. We want to run the country, and what the corporations are doing is what they should be doing in normal circumstances. They won't be constructive and they don't intend to be.

b) THE CIVIL RIGHTS MOVEMENT IN THE US

Clearly, the way in which the US Government and US-based firms behave toward and inside South Africa constituted the most important element in the overall evaluation Black South Africans make of the US. Their behavior in Africa and the Third World are also of relevance, and this will be looked at in Chapter 8. Of lesser importance, but still of significance to evolving Black perceptions, are their assessments of the domestic situation in the US.

QUESTION: Do you think that the Civil Rights Movement in the United States was a success?

Asked - 64; Positive - 38 (69% of those who gave an answer); Negative - 9; Conditional - 8; Don't know - 9.

QUESTION: What impression of the American political system does this leave you with? Are you positive or negative about the US political system?

Asked - 63; Positive - 32 (58% of those who gave an answer); Negative - 17; Conditional - 6; Don't know - 8.

Asking a question about their view on the Civil Rights Movement in the US, and a follow-up question on how this might influence their general perception of the US political system - did they view it in a positive light as a country which could solve problems of racial discrimination - provided an opportunity of discovering Black views on the US itself. The second question was phrased so as to indicate that they could, but did not have to, make a connection between their view of the Civil Rights Movement and that of the political system. The Civil Rights experience was clearly of some significance to them and most of those interviewed were familiar with it. It was also relevant to their thinking on race and class, on liberal democracy and social democracy and on the directions which they foresaw for their own struggle. The pair of questions also provided an opportunity for the US "to do well" in their eyes.

In fact it did so. It turned out to be the only question that elicited a response which could be said to be favorable to US policy and politics. A convincing majority felt that the Civil Rights Movement in the US was a success. A somewhat less convincing majority, but a majority nevertheless, went on to add that this left them with a positive impression of the US political system. (Responses were more positive in the second round of interviews.)

Amongst those who remained unimpressed by the results of the movement, the major themes were that it had misunderstood and, therefore, failed to alter power and social realities in the United States; or that it had made progress, but had retrogressed, or (this was not asked, but the response was forthcoming anyway) that it was not relevant to or was a false model for Black South Africans. For example, a trade union organizer (affiliated to Cosatu) felt that its poor record reflected a failure to distinguish between a bourgeois democracy and real (presumably popular) democracy. At a little more length, a senior person connected with the Nactu unions explained his view:

> Look at the current position. All the advances made by Martin Luther King are being rolled back and the clearly discernible signs are that if the US Government could dismantle the equal opportunities program it would. My impression is that the Civil Rights Movement failed to understand the make-up of political power in the US; that's what they should have aimed at, should have attempted to understand and build coalitions; now they are outflanked by the majority Whites, and minority interests are ignored.

A young man involved in an informal education program said he used to see it as a success and looked up to America; but now he had read of exploitation and poverty in America and no longer saw it in a positive light. Others acknowledged that it had succeeded on its own terms, but argued that these terms had amounted to misguided objectives. A man in his late 20's, whose work involved provision of legal advice to those in need, said:

> It was successful in what it intended to do. The problem is the way we view racism in the States. Racism is still alive. American society has a long way to go in resolving racism. It had a degree of success. From a socialist point of view, the question is can one eradicate racism under capitalism? ... since capitalism is irrational, racist and exploitative. Can one get rid of racism when it suits capitalism?

Along the same lines, an Azapo student argued:

> Viewed from a free enterprise system point of view, they have succeeded. Material life has improved. On the other hand, from a socialist point of view it was a Civil Rights movement, not a movement to enhance the material position of lower sections of the Black people. So if we evaluate it on its own terms it was a success. It advanced bourgeois interests. But it did not challenge fundamental relations in American society.

A middle-aged academic, a supporter of UDF, brought in the "South African analogy" factor:

> We have tremendous respect for Martin Luther King. ... But we understand that they can't produce the kind of social change we need ... so it does not represent the ideals to which we strive. I do not have a positive approach to the American political system. I would see it as a betrayal of the workers if the American system was brought here.

As did a journalist:

> It had an impact. It has improved the situation [of Black Americans] significantly and one hears Black voices quite a lot on very important issues, especially on foreign policy. But I am not really positive. As long as America is capitalist my belief is that capitalism owes its success to oppression; somebody must be oppressed. If Americans can't oppress Black people inside, they will have to do it elsewhere.

An educationist in Durban remained unimpressed by the system because the extension of political rights was on the basis of the "big guys" continuing to run America and not on the terms of the poor people. A community organizer in Soweto said that while it was better than South Africa there were worrying issues still in the form of the continuation of poverty, slums, a high crime rate and promiscuity in the wealthiest country in the world.

A self-employed man in Port Elizabeth judged the Civil Rights Movement a success but said he worried about Black Americans seeing parallels with South Africa which he said was a "very different kettle of fish." "Here marches won't work. We are not fooled by what happened there." An ex-union organizer and now middle-level manager, praised the thoughts of Martin Luther King Jr and Malcolm X and the progress of the Movement, but ended that he was nevertheless "not too enthusiastic about their system." Another middle-level manager, who combined extensive anger at US actions in South Africa with praise for the US political system, praised American Blacks for "pulling themselves up by their bootstraps," and praised the American system for its Bill of Rights, but concluded: "This is why we hate Americans more. They should know better." Others also attacked US policy in South Africa but praised the US Constitution, its system of checks and balances etc. A priest in Grahamstown was positive about the Movement and the political system.

> We see it as being successful. We know that Black people still suffer discrimination, but it is not discrimination by law; and we know that beatings and killings in the South have stopped. We know it is not perfect. But we really believe it is an improvement. It is an indication of a good political system.

A young official of Inkatha saw it as very successful, evidenced by the absence of segregation and discrimination on the statute books, and illustrating a good political system. An older colleague of his in Inkatha was also positive but added that it could go no further because of the control of big capital. "It has stopped now." A senior executive in a private firm praised the Movement:

> It had lessons for us. There are some similarities between South Africa and the US. Boesak and Tutu remind one of the church groups - very reminiscent of Martin Luther King's crusade. The church was used increasingly as an instrument of influencing policies. The universities here also show certain similarities. However, the harshness of the forces of reaction is so vehement here that it quickly radicalizes these people who would otherwise have looked for passive resistance rather than other alternatives. It

> gave America a conscience. They won't forget because they are now sensitive to issues bordering on racism. There is a general awareness of the moral injustice of race. It has been successful. They have not won a victory yet; but some major battles. I do admire their system.

A couple of Cape Town trade unionists were impressed by the publicity given the Iran-Contra hearings and by the fact that President Reagan could be defeated by Congress over sanctions. A Port Elizabeth priest commented that the US Government was not as "stubborn as this one;" and a Grahamstown school teacher spoke favorably of the right of peaceful protest in America. Finally, a Durban public interest lawyer commented positively:

> It is a good system. This is to a very large extent because of the checks and balances of the Constitution and the safeguards for the individual. Also because the Supreme Court is independent and has testing power. It can set aside decisions of Congress and the President - unlike in this country. Here some liberal judges try to arrive at justice by administering unjust laws.

In terms of non-governmental factors influencing perceptions of the US, corporations were judged negatively and the Civil Rights Movement positively. While there was some acknowledgement that American companies had improved their working conditions in recent years there was a general feeling that this had occurred only in response to pressures and threats both in South Africa and in the US. This left most people somewhat skeptical of the real intentions of these companies; although a sizeable minority still thought that it was possible - unlikely, but possible - that they could yet be a positive force for change. This would be feasible only if the changes Blacks sought were limited to an alteration of a racial character, and not if it included more radical economic consequences. As far as the Civil Rights Movement was concerned there was a fairly realistic assessment of both its successes and its limitations; it had brought progress to Black Americans but had stopped a substantial way short of being a victory. Although it was not seen as a model of relevance to the South African situation, it led to a positive judgement of the American political system's ability to deal with a serious political and ethical challenge. Some compared it favorably with South Africa, which is a very limited form of compliment. Once again there was little naivete about the perfection of the American system - and its problems were enumerated - nevertheless overall it was seen by the majority of the group in a positive light.

INTERNATIONAL ISSUES

As a further method of testing the nature of radicalization and of changing attitudes toward the United States, a list of six international relations questions were put to the interviewees. They were all questions high on the agenda of US foreign policy concerns and also dealt with matters about which at least some of the group would be familiar. In fact, the degree of familiarization with some of the issues was presumed in itself to provide some measure of growing conscientization among Black South Africans.

a) CUBANS IN ANGOLA

This issue was so close to home for Black South Africans that it was really both of domestic and international relations concern. More than the other questions the various ramifications of this one require explanation. When a politically divided Angola became independent in 1975 under a Marxist-oriented MPLA, South Africa, anticipating United States-C.I.A assistance, invaded Angola in an attempt to overthrow the new Government. The MPLA brought Cubans in to assist them in the defence of the country. The South Africans did not get

US assistance, because of a (post-Vietnam influenced) Congressional amendment prohibiting covert US operations in Angola. As a result, South African troops were forced to retreat to the south of Angola from where they continued a three-pronged strategy: logistical and military support to Jonas Savimbi's Unita movement, the main opposition to MPLA, raids aimed at the MPLA Government, and attacks on the South West African People's Organization (Swapo) camps, all adding up to a draining destabilization of Angola. In talks about the future independence of Namibia (sandwiched between Angola and South Africa) the South African Government made the departure of Cuban troops from Angola a prerequisite for progress, a linkage accepted by the Reagan Administration. In 1985, Congress decided to lift the ban on military assistance to forces in Angola, President Reagan welcomed to Washington, and praised very highly, Savimbi, and America began to send arms to Unita. The Unita leader has openly allied himself with the South African Government by, amongst other things, attending the formal opening of the South African Tricameral Parliament, something which most Black organizations in South Africa had fought hard to oppose. This was a case therefore where the US had put itself into a clear alliance with South Africa in supporting Savimbi. In the US the Cuban presence was generally presented as an example of a proxy intervention by the Soviet Union in an African nation.

QUESTION: What do you think of the presence of the Cubans in Angola?

Asked - 84; Positive - 56 (78% of those who gave an answer); Negative - 9; Conditional - 7; Don't know - 12.

A very large majority of the interviewees were positive (in general, very positive) about the Cuban presence, seven were conditional and only nine people were opposed. These nine were made up of six Inkatha followers, a very conservative manager, a businessman, and an otherwise rather radical community worker. The manager referred to expressed his criticism in the following way: "As much as I hate US imperialism, similarly I hate communist involvement. This is a threat to stability in southern Africa." A senior Inkatha official said the Cubans were not welcome and should go home. A young Inkatha officer said the Cuban presence worried him a lot.

> If Angola has a problem it belongs to the people of Angola. They don't need outside help. If Unita is stronger let Unita run the country. It is wrong for Cuba to run the country on behalf of the people.

Another member of Inkatha was critical, but, interestingly, for the opposite reason: namely that the Cubans were not doing anything effective. In his view, they should attack Savimbi and help Angola get rid of Unita, rather than simply acting as a line of defence against South Africa.

The "conditional" answers expressed concern about the size of the Cuban presence, the strain it caused on the Angolan Government's resources, and the seeming "permanence" of their stay, but in general were positive about their protecting Angola from attack by South African forces.

The very strong support for the Cuban military presence was based mainly on the threat of South Africa (and, a few added, of the US) to Angola, and on the full right of a sovereign government to invite whomever it wanted to help defend the country. A middle-aged woman professional thought that 60% of Blacks were pleased the Cubans were in Angola because "the enemy of my enemy is my friend." A woman academic added warmly: "They have come home and I'm glad they are remaining."

In terms of reasons for support given, answers proceeded from the usual anti-South Africa standpoint: "If it worries South Africa, good," to a minimalist technical position based on the right of Angola as a sovereign state to invite the Cubans, to the necessity of keeping South Africa out of Angola (they definitely saw South Africa and the US as aggressors, and not Cuba and the Soviet Union) - "otherwise Pretoria would turn Angola into another Lesotho" - to the need to defeat Savimbi, about whom very great distaste was expressed by many, to the conviction that the MPLA was the Government of the people of Angola, to support for the ideological commitment of the MPLA to socialism and justice, and (this included only a few of answers) to support for the nature of the Cuban Revolution and the hope that Cuba and Angola would benefit mutually from this common experience.

Strong negative emotions were expressed in these responses about Savimbi, Unita and US support for Unita. While doing interviews at Witwatersrand University, the Conservative Students' Union was distributing around the campus glossy magazines in support of Savimbi. Since this was during the state of emergency, nobody was allowed to respond, which added to the anger felt by students towards him. The incident during which some Unita officials were prevented from speaking on the campus has already been mentioned. In addition, US aid to Unita was raised by a good number of the group in response to other questions about their negative assessment of America. During the second round the proportion of them expressing support for the Cuban presence grew.

A student in Grahamstown said that he wished only that the Cubans could have got to Lesotho in time to prevent the South African instigated coup in that country. A Cape Town student was also very positive:

> The C.I.A. and the South African Government destabilize the African continent. They want to prove that the Angolan revolution failed. They want to show that capitalism is the best. They are trying to show that communism can't survive.

An academic gave his views on this:

> The American view of Namibia concerning the linkage of the Cubans to independence is totally unacceptable to us. We very much welcome their presence. They are defending the kind of societal change we want to see. There is a Xhosa song thanking the Soviets and the Cuban people for all they have done. It has become clear that no social and economic problems can be solved through Parliament here. Armed struggle, strikes, boycotts have become necessary to bring about change. The state of emergency is crushing democratic organization. So our people turn elsewhere. The parties which will help us are the Cubans, Russians, East Germans, Angolans, etc. America is making a fundamental mistake by not forcing the South African Government to lift the state of emergency. So we have no choice but to turn to the East. We get no support from Governments like Britain and the US.... So we welcome the Cubans.

One other point, observed by a few of the respondents including the academic just quoted, related to the "linkage" argument mentioned above; that is that Pretoria would not move toward giving independence to Namibia until the Cubans were out of Angola. The point was made that "the Cubans" were simply "an anti-communist strategy" used by Pretoria and "swallowed" by the Reagan Administration to delay indefinitely Namibia's independence.

It is necessary to point out that these interviews took place before the US-sponsored peace agreement on Namibia.

b) COLONEL QADDAFI

QUESTION: What is your opinion of Libya's Colonel Qaddafi?

Asked - 83; Positive - 31 (46% of those who gave an answer); Negative - 21; Conditional - 15; Don't know - 16.

Possibly no national leader elicits as much emotionally negative assessment in the US as Libya's Colonel Qaddafi. President Reagan attacked him consistently and in the strongest terms as a supporter of terrorism; in the end ordering a bombing raid on Libya, which included an attack on the home of Qaddafi.

Qaddafi is seen as a highly controversial figure in the third world, variously judged as heroic, unorthodox, irresponsible or dangerous. This was not a question that originally was on my list. In early discussions, however, I heard that in the townships young Blacks sang songs of praise to him and that in Soweto pro-Qaddafi graffiti could be found. The question was therefore added. The Libyan leader received a mixed reception from this group of Black South Africans. Nevertheless, the majority of those who took a side on this gave him a positive assessment.

Half of those who criticized him did so along lines familiar in the West: that he was "irresponsible," a "latter-day Idi Amin," a "buffoon," "crazy," "unpredictable" or "a little bit mad." One young man in Durban said: "As a member of Inkatha and a Zulu I just can't see how I can hero-worship a person who goes out to kill." Another young man in Durban, a supporter of the left of UDF, criticized his interventions on behalf of international terrorism, arguing that this provided Black South Africans with a poor example. A Ph. D. student noted that at the Non-Aligned Conference held in Harare, Zimbabwe, he had been both out of line with the majority and unwelcome. A Cape Town trade unionist attacked his interference in Egypt and Chad, his sponsoring of so many political splinter groups, the recklessness with which he operated, and the shooting of a woman police officer in England with no reported action against the perpetrator.

The other half of his critics, all trade unionists, did not comment on Qaddafi's foreign policies or refer to his state of mind, but criticized him for the lack of worker democracy in Libya. This reduced to about a dozen the number of those who would censure him for the same reasons as he is disparaged in Washington.

A number of those who said they held a positive view of Qaddafi based this on his stand against America. "I like him," said one middle-aged woman in the Eastern Cape, "because he put his finger in America's eye." One youth organizer, also in the Eastern Cape, said that while he did not agree with Qaddafi's Islamic Socialism he admired him for standing up to the US. "We sing songs about him as a hero of Africa. He is not mad. He is not the monster the media make him out to be." A middle-level manager returned to the "friend of a friend" theme: "To us he is a good symbol that a small country can stand up for itself. He has bad comments about South Africa, so he is a friend. The Arab countries are against South Africa and therefore they are our friends. He is against America and America jeopardizes us; so he is a good friend."

A number of people confirmed that his status had risen considerably as a result of the bombing raid on Libya; it turned him into a "hero." Also, shortly after the US raid, Pretoria engaged in bombing attacks on neighboring states. When reprimanded by the West, South Africa expressly made the comparison between the American need to bomb "terrorists" in Libya and South Africa's similar need to bomb "terrorists" in southern Africa. This analogy, too, added to his status. In addition, the fact that Washington refers to him as a terrorist in a similar way to Pretoria's reference to the ANC as terrorists led a young businessman to surmise that "Qaddafi probably is on the side of liberation." A few people added the point that Libya had helped with the training of South African liberation fighters, particularly those of the PAC. Some also commented that there was particularly strong empathy with Qaddafi amongst Moslems in Natal and the Western Cape. A Moslem professional had this to say:

> We [he was not limiting his comments to Moslems only] are positive about both Qaddafi and Khomeini. We see them both in a good light. We see the negative information spread about them as essentially the duplicity of the West - they manipulate this for their own selfish interests. Their stand is on religious grounds. I don't understand what exactly they are after, but the fact that they take on the West has our support. The more the West tries to denigrate them the more support we give.

Along the same lines a journalist remarked:

> We hear so many negative things said by our oppressors, that we find it difficult to believe. The more they condemn him the more we see him as a hero. We could be wrong but this is how we see it. We know that in Libya people are not suffering like they suffer here. In many countries condemned by capitalists people don't suffer as much as here. As long as we are prevented from gaining access to the literature about Libya we will continue to hero worship Qaddafi.

c) ISRAEL

In looking into Black attitudes towards Israel there are a number of components of the question that need to be kept in mind. First, there is the close association between Israel and the US. Second, there are the various aspects - trade, investment, security - of its relationship with South Africa. Third, there are the Arab-Israeli and Palestinian-Israeli conflicts. And fourth, there is the role of Jews in South Africa and the close connection between South African Jews and Israel. Singly, or in combination, these could affect perceptions of Israel. Although I did not ask interviewees to compare their present feelings with those of about 15 years ago, it would be my guess that Israel was probably held in quite high esteem by a fair number of non-Moslem Black South Africans. This would be a consequence of Israel's early public stance against apartheid, its well-publicized and effective aid program in Africa, the tendency of Black South Africans to see a natural ally amongst people who had also suffered so severely because of discrimination, a recognition that Jews in South Africa represented a disproportionately high percentage of liberal supporters and some of the economic and agricultural achievements of the new state. If this were so, those sentiments have clearly changed.

QUESTION: What is your view of Israel?

Asked - 83; Negative - 49 (73% of those who gave an answer); Positive - 3; Conditional - 15; Don't know - 16.

Only three of the group approved of Israel; two were members of Inkatha, and the third was a politically conservative manager. A young man said he "liked Israel a lot," particularly its capacity for survival. Another, an urban political organizer, commented:

> I am positive about Israel. It is a small nation that can bring itself together. They don't want to interfere with other countries. They only deal with issues that pertain to them. And they have made great technological progress.

A third Inkatha person was more mixed in his evaluation. While he appreciated the help which Israel had given to KwaZulu and the inspiration Israel provided as a country that had made it the hard way, he nevertheless disparaged Israel's military help to the apartheid system and its failure to unambiguously condemn apartheid. A few others, who were critical of Israel, still pointed to the kibbutz as something which they admired. For the rest, Israel was very negatively assessed.

The most common criticism was of its close ties with South Africa and the Pretoria Government. Israel's trade with South Africa was seen as being of significant advantage to the Israeli economy, and it was confidently anticipated by a few people that if and when economic sanctions were initiated, Israel would act as a main agent in breaking the effects of sanctions. There was also angry comment on Israel's assistance to, trade with, and investment in, the Bantustans, the Ciskei in particular. This was seen as giving political and economic support both to Pretoria and to the Homeland leaders, and also taking advantage of the extremely cheap labor available in those areas. There was strong condemnation of Israel's close military and security ties with Pretoria, the main impact of which was seen as impeding Black liberation.

An experienced lawyer commented: "Following the treatment of the Jews in Germany, that Israel now identifies itself with a racially oriented regime is totally inexplicable to me." A senior academic explained his feelings:

> I have great sympathy with Jews because of the Nazi history and because Jews have identified with the struggle for change in South Africa.... On the other hand, Israel is clearly seen as identifying with the South African Government, for example in circumventing the arms boycott and in exchanging military information. Israel will act as a conduit for arms and other commodities on behalf of Britain and the US when sanctions tighten up. Israel is in alliance with the South African Government. There is also a growing sympathy here for the Palestinians, certainly among the Moslems.

Almost word for word, a Cosatu organizer repeated these sentiments. Both a realization of parallels with the Palestinian issue, and sympathy for the Palestinian cause did seem to be on the increase. A young UDF supporter in the Eastern Cape said:

> I have strong views on this and these have not changed. I agree that Jews should have a place to live. But they had no right to take the Palestinians' land away. So they don't have a right to be there. We do identify our cause with that of the PLO and see our oppression as similar. Also the PLO supports us; so this grows.

Others mentioned further points of parallel; for example, of both peoples having been dispossessed of their land, of attempts in both cases at separate homelands solutions, at close alliances with America and capitalism, and as both serving on behalf of the West as "anti-communist buffers" in their regions. Moslem interviewees expressed this most strongly. A professional man maintained that he was totally against Israel:

> I have always been anti-Zionist and pro-PLO. Palestine was their country. Western duplicity dispossessed these people of their land and interjected foreign Jews - like a 53rd state of the United States - as a destabilizing factor in the Middle East. There is a very close analogy with South Africa; also a military nexus with the South African Defence Force they exchange their methods and equipment of torture with each other. Also, Israel has cornered the market in the Ciskei.

A Cape Town trade unionist castigated Israel for its treatment of Palestinians on the West Bank and in Gaza. "Their murderous tactics and their sledgehammer methods of bulldozing houses and bombing suspects has caused outrage."

> Israel's relations with South Africa in the light of the Jewish history of persecution is perplexing. It is an immoral relationship. For others to sell arms to South Africa is a problem, but for Israel to do that is a greater disappointment because of its peculiar position.

In the main, interviewees took trouble to point out that they were criticizing Israel, and not Jews. There were four people, three of them young Azapo supporters, who included in their reactions their attitudes towards Jews in South Africa. One pointed out that, in South Africa, Jews were "stinkingly rich" and that many sent their money to support Israel. "A big question is whether the Jews will share their wealth with the people after the change." A second person explained his position in this way:

> Israel is no different than America. The war with the PLO is an unjustifiable war. I wish it could be resolved. Jews are terrible. They are very strong in this country. Jews here at Wits [Witwatersrand University] are too strong. The Jews in Israel are the worst thing that ever came and they are annihilating people there. I pray for their defeat.

A third speaker referred specifically to the Black American Muslim leader who has been attacked in the US as being anti-Semitic:

> As the Reverend Farrakhan has said, Israel was founded on an injustice, and it will never know peace because of that. I don't believe Arab countries have the right to annihilate Israel. Israel and the Arabs should settle this. It is an illegal country.

d) US ROLE IN NICARAGUA

QUESTION: What do you think of American action toward Nicaragua?

Asked - 79; Negative - 53 (95% of those who gave an answer) ; Positive - 2; Conditional - 1; Don't know - 23.

This was the first of the questions that was really foreign in the sense that there was no direct link with South Africa. As a result, one finds here a higher proportion of people who were unfamiliar with the situation. But of those who did know about it, almost every one condemned the US actions in Nicaragua; whether or not they were strongly supportive of the Sandinistas, they saw it as an unjustified intervention by the US in Nicaragua. The terms "arrogant," "aggression," "imperialism," and "destabilization" were used to describe their views on this topic. It was seen as "overkill" perpetrated against a small, impoverished country which was too weak to provide a base for the spread of socialist revolution; as a continuation of a right-wing capitalist policy which had previously bolstered the Somoza Government and was now using ex-Somoza people to destabilize the Sandinistas. A Nactu-affiliated union organizer commented:

> Our view is supportive of all people trying to find their own identity and establish their own political structures for their own societies. We reject imposed solutions by whomever, from Pretoria or Washington.

A young woman who worked for a voluntary organization had attended a lecture by a woman who had stayed in Nicaragua for a month. She had told her audience of how people struggled to make a living and that the Americans were prevailing on countries not to buy products from, or give assistance to,

Nicaragua. A second person, a young labor research officer, had also spent time with people who had worked there:

> I am supportive of the Sandinistas. I have information from friends who worked there. I am impressed by the way they are trying to transform their society. There are lots of questions they haven't looked at yet, for example, the use of chemicals in agriculture, and they have a long way to go in deepening consciousness about a lot of issues. But I am very impressed by the way in which they are trying to resolve these issues.

A senior person in the banking business saw a connection with South Africa:

> I relate it very closely to our situation here. Reprisals and punitive measures there can be used here. Also, it is very odd of Reagan. Why doesn't he use the same arguments about sanctions hurting people in Nicaragua as he does when stopping sanctions on South Africa?

And a journalist also saw links:

> America is doing in Nicaragua what South Africa is doing in Angola. I can't understand how America can say South Africa must end apartheid when America is financing Unita and Unita is engaged in a fight aimed at perpetuating apartheid. So I can't find justification for America being involved in Nicaragua.

The principal source of annoyance seemed to be that a new Government of a small country was attempting to initiate reforms and was being prevented from achieving improvements because of US intervention. A man employed in a trade union support agency analyzed the action in this way:

> I am very critical. But it is not unexpected. America always subverts progressive governments and anti-imperialist governments which seek relations with socialist countries. America immediately becomes hysterical, and even more than hysterical when it is in America. The Bay of Pigs fiasco is an example of what the US can do when they feel that communism is at their doorstep.

A young educationist was one of four or five who expressly asserted strong support for the Sandinista revolution:

> This is very important to us. We find their revolution very romantic and take it very seriously: the military part of the struggle, the fight in rural areas, their treatment of women, are all seen very positively. Again, what America is doing there influences our attitude toward the US. It has no right to interfere and support the Contras.

And lastly, a university research associate warned that the same thing could happen in South Africa in the future; if there were a "government of the people the US will interfere so as to ensure the freedom of capitalism to continue exploiting people."

e) THE SOVIET ROLE IN AFGHANISTAN

QUESTION: What is your opinion of the Soviet role in Afghanistan?

Asked - 79; Negative - 40 (74% of those who gave an answer); Positive - 5; Conditional - 9; Don't know - 25.

Three-quarters of those who answered were critical of the Soviet action in Afghanistan and a number commented that they opposed both US imperialism in Nicaragua and Soviet imperialism in Afghanistan. As a BC union organizer said: "there must be a feeling of moral equivalence." Yet in comparison with views on US actions in Nicaragua, there were five who were positive about the Soviet role and nine who gave conditional answers (as compared to two positives and one conditional on the American case) and, more significantly, the tone of the criticism was more muted.

The strongest censure came from Inkatha and Azapo supporters. An official of the former said:

> The presence of the USSR worries me. The USSR will be there for its own gain, political and monetary. I know of no country that the Soviet Union has come into and left that country afterwards. They are draining the wealth, for example, of Mozambique. Mozambique has definitely not become Utopia. The Soviet Union helped them become independent, but no more.

And the Azapo/BC supporters made clear their distaste for Moscow's actions by stressing the equivalence of the two situations:

> As much as I challenge America in Nicaragua I will also condemn the invasion of Russians in Afghanistan and Poland. Any defeat of America is a victory for the Third World, but there is a tendency by the Russians to colonize, to be imperialist. We don't want Russia to be the representative of the people of South Africa.

So one has here a rare agreement between Black Consciousness and Inkatha. BC - and PAC - have always been concerned about the influence of the South Africa Communist Party in the ANC and of the possibility of too close relations with the Soviet Union. This has long been a point of conflict between PAC and ANC. Even in its more Marxist form Black Consciousness remains opposed to Soviet influence and this is evidenced by the undiluted criticism of Soviet action in Afghanistan. Inkatha's comprehensive pro-Western and anti-Communist approach explains its position.

For the rest, respondents were in the main critical, but for various, reasons reservations were expressed about outright condemnation. First, and typically, there was concern about the purpose of the South African media in reporting on the conflict. A university student councillor communicated his concern in this way:

> Any news from South Africa worries me. If South Africa tells me the Russians are interfering in Afghanistan I know they are overplaying it. I scarcely believe anything bad about Russia because I hear it from the wrong sources. The South African press has succeeded in teaching Black people to read anything they say in reverse. Not just to read between the lines, but the reverse.

Then there was a general uncertainty about the facts. As a Bishop said, "it is too far away from my own experience". Others also said they did not have the full story. A couple of people noted that it had been a source of concern but as an issue it had faded away and people were not talking about it much any more. A businessman put forward two further reasons: "The Russians worry us less because they don't profess to be champions of freedom and because people see the East as our friends and are therefore less critical." This point about the Soviet Union's support for liberation in South Africa (and elsewhere) was made by a few people. Only a small number in the group argued the case that the Soviet Union had been invited in by the Afghanistan Government. One was a young UDF supporter in the Eastern Cape; another a senior UDF supporter in Natal, who said:

> This is a very complex question. I believe they were invited by a duly elected government. Then a section of the population revolted against it. I don't see the Russians as intervening. It is the same as the Cubans in Angola, that is, they were invited in to resist invasion by South Africa. Pakistan and the US keep the conflict alive by their support.

A third was a trade unionist who commented:

> It is tricky, but I am positive. There is a world struggle between capitalism and socialism. We are involved in a way between the two powers. The tendency is for people here and the media here to see America in Nicaragua, Grenada, and El Salvador portrayed as defenders of democracy; but they are really defending capitalist interests. The same media project what is happening on the other side in such a way as to make people believe that socialism is not working, that it is totalitarian, dictatorial, etc. So we know they want to equate the two. The two involve-

> ments are qualitatively different. One is to defend capitalism. The other is to help defend the small gains of socialism. This is what the Soviet Union is doing. The decision to call in the Soviet Union was by the Government of Afghanistan. It is not like the American invasion of Grenada.

The contrast between assessments of US action in Nicaragua and Soviet action in Afghanistan is subtle (it is about tone and degree) but nevertheless real. Soviet aid to the ANC would provide one reason. Suspicion of media reporting definitely provides a second. And a greater distance from the realities of the Soviet Union would serve as a third. This comparative point is significant; but it should not be overstressed. The key point is that the large majority of the group opposed the Soviet action.

It is necessary to point out that this question were asked before the Soviet withdrawal from Afghanistan commenced.

f) POLISH GOVERNMENT ACTION AGAINST SOLIDARITY

QUESTION: What is your opinion of the action taken by the Polish Government against Solidarity?

Asked - 78; Negative - 37 (74% of those who gave an answer); Positive - 5; Conditional - 8; Don't know - 28.

In the first round of interviews, although a majority of those who knew sufficient to comment and take a particular view were critical of the Polish Government, the overall result amounted to even more mixed response than to the question on Soviet action in Afghanistan. Very few people were actually positive about the crushing of Solidarity, but adding those who felt positive with those who gave conditional answers one ended up with about equal numbers with those who criticized it. In the second round there was a dramatic increase in the proportion of those who held a negative opinion of the Polish Government action. The only explanation I might suggest for this derives from a point made in the first year - and dealt with below - that after a certain period of time, because of independent information, people came to believe that the news they were receiving about official suppression of a workers' movement was accurate and not South African media propaganda.

Again one needs to understand the suspicion with which news presented by the Government and the press is viewed by Black South Africans. A young community organizer expressed his doubts:

> Again - as with the Afghanistan war - we were troubled because we were sympathetic to a trade union movement. But it faded. Also the South African Government and the US Government make so much of these issues for their own propaganda purposes that we become very suspicious and negative towards their propaganda.

He went on to emphasize suspicion of the South African media. A woman academic who sympathized with Solidarity expressed suspicion of all the good publicity Lech Walesa received and the continuous painting of Jaruzelski "as an ogre," and continued: "I suspect all the attention is given to this because White people are involved." Along somewhat similar lines a professional manager (overall one of the most supportive in the group of the US) said that he had been put off a bit by Reagan calling on the people of the US to burn a candle for Polish workers, "yet he never said a word about burning a candle for Black South African workers." Another concern was that Black South Africans should not take a stand on this issue as it could "bedevil our struggle" for example by exacerbating divisions between pro- and anti-Soviet people on the left. Furthermore, the same person observed "the Polish people in South Africa don't help us, so we don't have to sympathize with Solidarity. Also Solidarity did not identify with us and so we don't with them."

A further cause of doubt for some of the interviewees was based on the international support which Solidarity received. In other words Walesa's standing suffered because of the nature of his foreign allies. "He is supported by people who are our oppressors, the capitalist countries, and this raises a lot of suspicion." A Nactu-affiliated union organizer said:

> This is very tricky. At the level of worker grievances against what they did, I believe workers should be free to challenge. But at the level of interference by the imperialists giving support to Solidarity, we are put off. The Nobel Peace prize, for example, serves the interests of a particular perspective. Nkrumah would not have got it; Castro won't get it. It is not neutral. We do believe in worker democracy, but we have mixed feelings about this.

Another perspective held that while there was an initial validity to Solidarity's case it eventually brought the trouble down on itself.

> This is complex. There was a material basis for its existence. Poland is a socialist country. But socialism doesn't mean that all problems are solved in one stroke. Workers had genuine problems. But in terms of the struggle it is easy to abuse these problems, to heighten the conflict unnecessarily. This was not an imperialist sponsored problem, but as it unfolded it assumed new dimensions and became a political movement challenging state power.... Ultimately the Polish Government was forced to act to solve the problem.

Again one has an interesting division in viewpoints. In this case people on the right of this group and trade unionists (generally on the left) were the most strongly critical of the Polish Government. As with their assessment of Qaddafi, trade unionists based themselves on support for worker democracy and they therefore supported Solidarity. A young labor adviser with close association with the unions provided this background:

> This is a significant event in the socialist debate. What we see is a revolution inside a so-called socialist country. We thought it was not possible.... In the trade union movement we had access to a movie produced for the BBC which dealt with the worker occupations of the shipyards and the process of negotiation between Solidarity and the Polish Government. We were very impressed with the negotiation and with the strong democracy inside Solidarity and the broad support for Solidarity.... The event raises a lot of questions about one party being the supreme authority. This is very important to the unions here. We have used the films a lot. Originally we relied on the South African media and we were ready to believe it was a CIA or a Vatican plot. Subsequently we got our information independently and we saw it differently. We don't want to see Solidarity crushed. It is a question of the way in which socialism came to these countries. People will only defend something if they have participated in the transformation of the society. But in Poland it was imposed from without. Now the people were attempting to take control. What does democracy mean if people have no control over their destiny?

A BC-oriented unionist gave this interpretation:

> The trade union movement must be free, independent and democratic. If the state kills it, that must be opposed. There must be a lesson here. We cannot reject State interference in trade unions in South Africa and agree to it elsewhere. In 10 years time, if we have the ANC in control (with the support of the South Africa Communist Party) then we don't want them to interfere - it would not be tolerable.

And finally, an organizer of one of the Cosatu-affiliated unions explained:

> It was bad. It is talked about a lot. People are beginning to distinguish Russia and socialism and ask questions about the working class in those so-called communist countries. As a socialist I would defend the gains made in 1917, but it must be left to the workers to defend, not the bureaucrats.

Clearly, what was occurring here was a parallel debate- one relating to Poland and the other to a post-apartheid South Africa - and there was thus a combining of lessons learnt from Poland with justifications for union autonomy in both present-day and a post-apartheid South Africa. The BC-oriented unions would be ready to criticize the Soviet Union, and to assert an independence from a future ruling party which they might anticipate to be the ANC. Of more importance still, and this relates to a very significant internal debate, Cosatu unions which were supportive of ANC were also asserting that workers' trade unions must have autonomous existence outside of the main political party. Also significant was the consistent emphasis on worker democracy and participation: this emerges again in the next discussion.

The responses of this group to the questions on Angola and Nicaragua and also those on Israel and, in a more conditional sense, on Qaddafi, all add up to a very negative assessment of US foreign policy behavior particularly in the third world. There was considerable hostility contained in these answers and at least as much suspicion of the basic motives of American foreign policy in the analyses. There was also evidence of growing awareness of, conscientization about, and identification with other third world movements and societies seen as suffering directly and indirectly from US intervention; for example, the Nicaraguans, the Palestinians and the Angolans. On the other hand, they were aware of the issues and expressed opposition (not as acerbic but nevertheless clear) toward Soviet action in Afghanistan and the Polish Government's handling of the Solidarity movement. For a variety of reasons, including a sense of some gratitude to the USSR for its material aid to the ANC and a deep distrust of those who control news of international events and its interpretation, there was some reservation about censuring that behavior too strongly. But censure it 75% of them did.

VIEWS ON THE AFRICAN EXPERIENCE

Discussion so far has been based on responses to questions focused on perceptions of US policy toward South Africa, domestic Black politics in South Africa and a selection of international relations issues. This chapter introduces a further dimension, that of Black South African perceptions of Africa's post-colonial experience. Close to Black South Africans geographically and emotionally, it was thought that the African "factor" would also play into and influence views on international relations, the role of foreign powers, ideological orientations and visions of a post-apartheid South Africa.

a) MOST ADMIRED AFRICAN LEADERS

A few introductory points may be made about the responses to this question. The first one is that in general few of the group were very impressed by the record of African leadership. A young Inkatha officer said that while he admired the speeches they made and their courage "in finding liberation" he did not "know of one who runs his country well." Others echoed this point about disillusionment with African leaders in general. Secondly, there seemed to be little familiarity with most of the earliest generation of post-colonial African Presidents and Prime Ministers. Thirdly, most of the group were knowledgable

QUESTION: Please name the African leader whom you most admire?

	(1986)	(1987)	Total
Mugabe (Zimbabwe)	15	13	28
Nyerere(Tanzania)	15	9	24
Kaunda (Zambia)	12	8	20
Machel (Mozambique)	2	8	10
Kenyatta (Kenya)	6	1	7
Nkrumah (Ghana)	4	3	7

about, and interested in, leaders in geographically more proximate countries. And fourthly, attitudes were influenced as much, probably more so, by the leaders' contributions to the South African liberation struggle, as by their effectiveness at home. And so, the answers concentrated on three figures, all important members of the Front Line States, all closely concerned with the cause of Black South Africans. A priest's response summed this up:

> I admire Kaunda, Nyerere and Mugabe. This is mainly because they have been consistent in their support of liberation forces in southern Africa. Even if they have suffered they have kept on. Also we admire them because they have been seeking an alternative way forward, different from capitalism. My admiration is more to do with the first than the second.

Nyerere is probably the only African leader who was widely respected because of his performance as a leader per se (that is, not only because he has been a consistent supporter of liberation movements). A pro-capitalist, conservative manager said he admired Nyerere because he was "progressive, honest, open-minded and sympathetic with the South African cause. I don't care for his socialism though." An academic councillor's don't care for his socialism though." An academic councillor's respect for the Tanzanian leader was based on his honesty, simplicity and unassuming nature, and, in addition, that he had resisted moves to depersonalize Africans culturally. "I don't care that he did not succeed. He was serious about what he was doing, and not simply politicking." A technical assistant also acknowledged that Tanzania's socialism had been far from perfect but felt that Nyerere had "opened it up for all to see and to correct his mistakes." A couple of people added the point that a major reason for Nyerere's policies not working was that they were undermined by outside interference from the West, which wanted to ensure that they did not succeed. In short, despite what was seen as his economic failure, Nyerere's honesty, integrity and his serious and sincere experiment with African socialism account for the admiration accorded him.

Robert Mugabe was admired by a greater number of the group. He was, however, considerably more controversial: as will be seen he was also disparaged by some of those interviewed. He was far and away the most discussed African leader. His predicament, as a Black leader of an African state in which a minority White regime had been forced to hand over power, was seen as closely analogous to, and relevant for, a possible future South African scenario. He was being closely watched. A professional manager praised him for being honest, incorrupt, abstinent, unflamboyant and pragmatic. A businessman said that he had put White Rhodesian fears of the "unknown" to rest, and as such he had provided a very constructive example for South Africa. A banker commented that Mugabe's war and post-war example gave hope for South Africa: it need not be destroyed completely before liberation; it was possible to manage the economy and society even in the emotion of the immediate post-violence phase; and it was possible to restrain the high demands and anticipations of the victors. A journalist also respected Mugabe's record for the following reasons:

> He inherited a country in ruins. It seems he got it back into shape - in spite of the negative publicity his policies receive here. He has made compromises. But in a post-apartheid society we will also see that things turn out differently from the way we anticipate. When we are in control we will have to face up to realities. We will face obstacles. We too will have to be pragmatic.

His pragmatism, realism, "sensible" compromise with capitalism and reconciliation with Whites received praise from businessmen and managerial personnel, many of whom favored a strong private sector or at least a balanced system. But he also came in for considerable criticism (see following table), by all the trade unionists and a few others, for his suppression of worker rights, trade union activity and human rights. A young labor adviser gave this evaluation:

> To some extent I admire him. He is pretty articulate. But I don't actually approve of what is going on [in Zimbabwe]. There is very slow change. He is repressing the [opposition] Nkomo faction. You can't get a job without a ZANU-PF [the ruling Party] card. You can't openly support Nkomo. I don't like the way he deals with the trade union movement; for example, the banning of strikes. Zimbabwe is still a capitalist country.

These points about restrictions on worker freedoms and also imprisoning of trade union leaders were commented upon in a number of responses. This is an issue of significance which has already been raised in this Study. On different grounds he was censured by an Inkatha supporter:

> He supports violence in South Africa and this violence is Black on Black violence. He also talks about our leader [Buthelezi] badly without knowing the facts about what our leader is doing and the extent of support he has. We don't want Mugabe calling him a sell-out, a puppet.

The third leader whose name was frequently mentioned was President Kaunda of Zambia. This positive perception was based almost totally on his consistent support over many years for all the liberation wars in Mozambique, Angola, Zimbabwe and South Africa, and in appreciation of the suffering that Zambia had experienced in consequence. An academic commented:

> Zambia is not perfect. It is not engaged in the social reform we had expected. But it may not have been possible given the country's social and economic circumstances. But it has supported us, and its intentions are to have fundamental reform. I don't want to criticize.

The few people who did make observations on Kaunda's performance as a national leader were negative.

The late President Kenyatta of Kenya was mentioned favorably by seven people: for leading his people to independence, for good leadership, for uniting Kenya and keeping it stable and prosperous. On the other hand, he received four negative assessments: for permitting corruption in government, for allowing gross disparities in income so that "independence does not mean anything for the man in the street," and for "hijacking the people's movement and subordinating the struggle [of the Mau Mau] to his own interests." In 1987 he received only one positive comment compared to six the previous year. I have no explanation for this.

Samora Machel of Mozambique, by contrast, gained in standing - 8 positives and 2 negatives in 1987 as compared to 2 positives and 6 negatives in 1986. In the first round of interviews he came in for criticism. The word "disappointed" in the question was key to the response. He was not being criticized in the same way as Amin or Banda, but very specifically because he had raised very high hopes and then taken an action which many Black South Africans felt was a letdown. The victory of Frelimo in Mozambique, with those in Angola and also Guinea-Bissau, had provided a source of inspiration to

Black South Africans, particularly young people. In addition, Machel's charisma, his leadership of a successful war of liberation and his radicalism had provided a new and very exciting factor in southern Africa. In 1984, however, his economy in very poor shape, to some extent a result of South African aggression, he had signed a non-aggression accord with South Africa, which meant that South African liberation forces would not be able to operate from Mozambique. This is what caused the disappointment. He was seen to have sold out. Some of the people pointed to floods and droughts as causes of his problems, others to South Africa's destabilization activities, and a couple to the failure of the Soviet Union to assist him when he was in need. Between the two rounds of interviews, Machel was killed when the airplane in which he was travelling flew off course and crashed inside the South African border. Many Blacks in South Africa would hold Pretoria responsible for his death; and clearly some were willing to understand his accord with South Africa and restore to him the high status which he had previously held.

Finally, a few people (mainly Black Consciousness supporters) made mention of the late Kwame Nkrumah of Ghana. He was seen as a great visionary and committed pan-Africanist. He was someone whose books they still studied and admired.

b) AFRICAN LEADERS WHO HAD MOST DISAPPOINTED

Little discussion was thought necessary to explain distaste for Idi Amin's role in Uganda: as one of Africa's most publicized disasters this was thought to be broadly understood.
Although far fewer people mentioned Bokassa of the short-lived Central African Empire, those that did also felt it unnecessary

---

QUESTION: Who is the African leader who has most disappointed you?

	(1986)	(1987)	Total
Amin (Uganda)	12	13	25
Banda (Malawi)	10	8	18
Mugabe (Zimbabwe)	5	4	9
Machel (Mozambique)	6	2	8
Bokassa (C Af Empire)	1	4	5

---

to expand on this. There were clear explanations, however, for the disappointment felt about President Kamuzu Banda of Malawi. A priest explained: "Banda is the most unpopular because he is the only one to send an ambassador to South Africa and he is openly friendly with South Africa and because of his dismal record on human rights at home." Someone else described him as a "megalomaniac," corrupt and a South African stooge, also, for turning Malawians into "begging sort of people who are very tame and timid." Another person complained that Banda was turning the people of Malawi into "what this system turned us into: the people of Malawi can't think for themselves. He is depersonalizing Black people." The responses, both favorable and unfavorable, about Mugabe and Machel have already been discussed.

c) LESSONS FROM TWO DECADES OF AFRICAN INDEPENDENCE

The following question was asked: Most of Africa has been independent for two decades and more now. What lessons have you learnt? Specifically, what problems would you like to avoid in the liberation and post-liberation process? And what policies would you wish to to see promoted?

There were a number of interesting responses to this question which did not specifically attempt to list concrete suggestions. One line of argument, here represented by an academic at the University of Natal, was that there was not anything so special about Africa "which makes it[s experiences] intangibly common between Africans."

> The nature of traditional societies, common ownership of land, family, community - all those are of marginal effect. We can learn from Africa and from the third world as a whole. But our landscape will be broader. Is it going to matter to me ... whether I draw lessons from India, China or Cuba? We have every hope of avoiding what has happened to Africa because South Africa's is a unique struggle for freedom in a highly industrialized country with a very large proletariat, and an increasingly aware proletariat and a very high level of leadership.

"I refuse to believe," was another response, "that what has happened in the post-colonial era will automatically happen here." An almost opposite line of argument was that there was no point in trying to learn lessons because South Africa would have to go through the same problems, since this was inherent in a situation in which the new leaders, as educated as they might be, would lack experience. "We must fumble and find our way. Like Zimbabwe we will have in-fighting. There are the PAC and the ANC; and Azapo can still cause trouble because Black Power is contrary to the ANC, and so on." A third angle on this was that the African experience had been so "pathetic" that there was nothing to learn. In general, there was no romanticism about the African experience, and most ideas seemed to emerge from what had gone wrong rather than successes. The exceptions were those people who admired Mugabe and believed there were positive lessons to be learnt from Zimbabwe.

One such lesson was the need to keep White people in the country, and to avoid decisions or policies which might scare them off: these included "nationalization," "too much nationalization," "oppression" and "moving too fast." An Inkatha officer cautioned against rhetoric about throwing Whites into the sea, and called for a multiracial society based on merit which instilled a love for all irrespective of race. A banker saw it in these terms:

> Mugabe is a great example. Machel, Kaunda and Nyerere, because of their adherence to extreme socialist principles, are a nightmare. Mugabe's inclusion of White technocrats in his administration is a good lesson. We should talk about power sharing here, not majority rule. We should learn to be as flexible as possible in our approach to the management of the economy.

A professional in a private corporation made a similar appeal not to lose "our technical personnel."

> We must keep this in mind when negotiating. We must not allow one nation to dominate. We need to have a role for Whites in Government or else we will frighten them off. We need to find a new structure because people in the minority are the ones with knowledge and the majority lack technology.

A manager in Port Elizabeth warned against scaring Whites off by taking away their houses and businesses, as long as they accepted a free political dispensation. He wanted land to be shared, but the mines should not be nationalized because Blacks did not have the necessary skills to manage them. While it was the education system that was at fault in denying Blacks technological expertise, nevertheless, top positions should remain in the hands of those who merited holding them and had the education to do so.

The other of the two more common themes was of a different kind and emanated from a different group of people: this stressed the need for worker's organizations to retain their independence from the dominant political party. A Cosatu-affiliated union organizer, pointing to the experience of workers under Mugabe, suggested that a political party may not be the right movement to lead the country to independence since there is a tendency for the party to "forget and oppress the worker as soon as independence comes." In his view, workers must therefore be much more central to the takeover of the state. And, he added, this was a problem throughout Africa. A second man, also from a Cosatu-related union said:

> Zimbabwe won a significant victory over colonialism. It reduced racial discrimination. There is a significant surge towards educating the people. But if we look at the workers' benefits, they are minimal. Workers are still exploited. Capitalism is still there. Maybe it is welfare capitalism but it is still there. In 1983 the Zimbabwe Government promulgated a law which is essentially anti-worker, making legal strikes very difficult. Workers have not reaped the benefits of independence. This was the important strategy. Lancaster House has paid off. And the reason is that during the liberation struggle the workers were not organized distinctively with their own clear ideology; also because in the guerrilla war the party strategy did not establish links with a worker strategy and worker organizations. Also, the working class was small. The important lesson is that Cosatu must say it is independent and stay independent.

A woman ex-trade union organizer made the general point that in Africa a handful of people were enjoying liberation when the majority had fought for it, and then went on to argue that "the workers are the most important people in the country. They deserve to run the country; they should determine conditions and wages to workers and who decides these things."

Third on the list of lessons was the need to avoid imperialism. An academic councillor argued that the first need was to keep away American, British and European imperialism, which had left Africa in the lurch and kept on draining Africa. "Dependence continues and when the African countries could not pay their debts, America forced them to devalue." A graduate student said:

> Third World countries are vulnerable to imperialist manipulation. Independence is nominal. To break away needs very disciplined people. But how? We are evolving out of the womb of imperialism, and they will forever keep us attached - this will lead to vulnerability, coups and corruption.

An Azapo official urged Blacks to take their struggle beyond mere anti-colonialism, for such a limited objective would lead to neo-colonialism and a loss of control over their own destiny and the chances of building a society based on socialism. A young UDF supporter added that care must be taken to avoid a negotiated settlement because that would prevent the total transfer of power to the working class and therefore the establishment of a socialist society.

Next on the list, although phrased in very different ways, was the need to emphasize democracy and participation and avoid political oppression, military governments, one-party states, dictatorships and personality cults. An Inkatha official said that "Democracy should be held high. We shouldn't oppress Whites. We must remember the importance of people-based development and avoid the one-party state." A professional manager said he was concerned that the oppression of the majority would throw up a new leadership that would itself in turn oppress, and he expressed the hope that Mandela would rise above this. There was criticism, by a few people, of what they described as the "far left" of the movement "influenced by Stalinism," that might try to force a one-party system on the country.

A good number of respondents, mainly in the second round of interviews, made urgent pleas for economic pragmatism. Whether the end result was intended to be socialism or a mixed economy, the call was to proceed step by step and avoid rushing into radical and potentially disturbing new economic policies. A school teacher contended that the Mozambican experience demonstrated the dangers of promising Marxism to the people and making too close contacts with, and too many promises to, the East. In his opinion, Marxism did not work out in the way it promised to and it seemed to lead to internal conflict, as in both Mozambique and Angola. He also mentioned the Ethiopian experiment as being unsuccessful. South Africa, he said, was a capitalist society and would need to operate as a mixed economy for at least ten years before moving towards some kind of socialism. A community activist in Uitenhage concluded that extreme radicalism and anti-Westernism had not helped African countries. "In the end we will need Western countries." A Durban professional, a supporter of UDF, who favored socialism in the long term, spoke of Africa rushing blindly into nationalization and socialism in an attempt to share wealth and reduce inequality. Zimbabwe had taken cognizance of this and was following a pragmatic path. The ANC, he felt confident, would act in similar fashion and there would be no mass nationalization. A lawyer expressed caution in the following terms:

> We must always be on our toes. If we decide to go for socialism then we should not go for it hook, line and sinker. Lots of developments still have to take place. We need to make assessments before trying to create a new kind of society based on a unique situation. In the meantime we need lots of education to gain the technical knowledge. We must get our human resources ready first.

A Cosatu-affiliated union organizer agreed with an analysis of a Soviet scholar, published in mid-1987, which urged Black South Africans to pursue democracy first and worry about socialism later.

A further area of concern was ethnicity. Since an emphasis on ethnicity as a divisive mechanism of apartheid has long been recognized, a stress on counteracting this has been at the core of all the more important liberation movements. A graduate student in Johannesburg who supported the UDF warned that ethnic divisions could render South Africa vulnerable to outside intervention:

> Ethnic divisions give imperialism a chance to come in. In kinship terms, if a neighbor realizes there is division and shouting in the family the neighbors will bewitch and kill you. It is the same here. If imperialists see divisions they will use the opportunity to sponsor the side they support as in Nigeria, Zaire and others.

Related to the general concern about ethnicity was a particular warning by opponents of Inkatha that Chief Buthelezi's stress on Zulu culture, traditions and identity represented the clearest danger, particularly because of his acceptance by White liberals and the US, which was based, in turn, on his identification with capitalism. In this regard, a woman manager in the Eastern Cape referred to Buthelezi's leadership as a curse, but warned that because of the Government's persistence with its homelands policy the danger was broader in nature. Examples were given of other Homeland leaders who were following Buthelezi's example and establishing their own ethnic-cultural organizations. A few others noted that ethnicity was not the only divisive force. There were ideological differences as well which were exacerbated by leaders' ambitions. "It is very important that we listen to each other." Indicative of the problem, the same speaker then launched into an attack on the BC-Unity movement which he said was sowing confusion by continually trying to discredit the ANC.

A further point, again phrased in diverse terms, was the danger of mistaking the shallow form of independence for genuine social change. A junior administrator in a voluntary organization stressed the need for "complete independence politically and economically as an essential base on which to build scientific socialism - not African socialism - and remain free of both superpowers." A Nactu-affiliated union organizer spoke of Kenya and Zambia, where the parties centered themselves on the leaders and forgot that it is not so much leaders that matter but a change in the system which brings equality. "Changing from Black to White is not the same as freedom."

> Kaunda's humanism, for example has not changed relationships. We must be sure that we do not bring about a situation in which a new master is warring against us.

A labor research officer in Durban saw the gravest danger in the failure to educate and involve grass roots supporters in the political education process. The trade union movement was doing this at the shop floor level, but this was still insufficient. There was a tendency to regard a person as politically educated if he or she knew the main points of the Freedom Charter and to call people "progressive" without defining the term or finding out if the people's analysis and activism conformed to progressive notions. People's understanding of concepts and debates must be increased, their access to decisions broadened, while movements like the UDF must consistently (and not erratically) work in a democratic manner. Otherwise, he felt, the revolution would lead simply to "seizure of the state and not to the restructuring of society." Others too stressed the need for both political and other education to prevent the new leadership from dominating the people. A couple of interviewees in the 1987 round introduced another item onto the educational agenda. A woman activist in Cape Town observed that the man in the street had not been prepared for the suffering that might follow after independence and they were led to believe that all would be wonderful. With this in mind a Cape Town trade union official warned:

> We must distinguish between the ideal and the practice. Independence might turn out to be miles apart from what the people fought for and what they envisaged in the struggle. One has to be aware of this possibility and be ready to deal with it; as in Mozambique. You may have independence and the situation may at first be worse than

> it was. So you need to prepare the people for that kind of situation, and not just be looking for excuses and scapegoats afterwards.

A Black Consciousness sympathizer pointed out the necessity for Black Consciousness to operate in the post-apartheid era because of the continuing danger of White cultural superiority and White skills and organizations reestablishing themselves. An unaffiliated unionist, sympathetic to the BC approach, called for the retention of some traditional African structures:

> Constitutional formulas implanted in Africa from outside will remain alien. Even African relief programs and self-help projects failed because they were not linked to African tradition and customs. There will be a major problem unless the PAC with its Africanist solutions has some influence. It may be reactionary but you can't automatically transfer a whole society from its traditional customary world to the existing one. It is essential to a peaceful transition. Our proud cultures must be upheld.

Finally an academic interweaved two further themes:

> We must totally change the security forces. In factories we can't leave the existing management in charge, because it won't bring change. We need to train new kinds of managers. But it will depend on the level the whole liberation struggle has reached. Zimbabwe was moving there; but peace terminated the revolutionary process. Also on education. How can we keep the same officials if we introduce "people's education?" We are in a liberation process and the instruments of a future government are there in embryo: street committees, factory committees, and in education. The process must be consciously prodded on because this is not simply a question of a Black take over. So much will depend on what is thrown up by the revolutionary process and at what stage of the revolutionary struggle we will be when change comes.

The most common reasons for admiring a leader were: 1) he liberated his country; 2) he consistently supported Blacks in South Africa; 3) he is pragmatic and reconciliatory; 4) he has ethical and intellectual qualities; 5) he has shown inspiring and effective leadership; and 6) he has created political stability. The three most common bases for criticism were 1) too close ties with Pretoria, 2) poor development performance, and 3) dictatorial and undemocratic behavior. There were a number of people who praised some leaders for their commitment to socialism and disparaged others for their backing of capitalism; but these types of answers were less common than those listed. Taken by themselves, these replies indicated a rather non-ideological preference for leadership that was ethical and effective in maintaining a democratic and stable political system and a pragmatic and successful economic system. This probably does indicate a certain level of pragmatism in the group; but it may also be a consequence of their judging that there were no successful models in Africa from which they could learn, and on which the interviewees might have based a convincing ideological or policy case. If, say, Machel's, Nyerere's and Mugabe's earlier stated policies had succeeded, socialists among Blacks in South Africa would have had helpful case studies on which to base their arguments. Similarly, no proponent of the free enterprise system felt that he or she could point to capitalist successes. Clearly there was some sympathy in the group for Nyerere's African Socialism and Mugabe's pragmatic mixed social welfare economy; but there was probably a more general feeling that South Africans needed to find a new way.

There was no very clear thrust either to the answers on lessons learnt from the African experience. Suggestions covered a wide spectrum. The following were raised most often as problems to *avoid*: economic dependence and imperialism, ethnicity, oppression, internal fighting and divisions of any kind, personality cults, a one-party state, anti-White rhetoric and policies, economic destruction, and worker oppression. And objectives which they wished to see *promoted*: keep Whites in the country, keep those with expertise, worker independence from the ruling party, relevant education (both to develop human resources and to increase understanding of future uncertainties), stability, democracy, pragmatic economic policies and pragmatic socialism. Probably the most important emphases were on retaining Whites, democracy, worker democracy, economic independence and pragmatic moves at least some way away from capitalism. Opinions were divided, sometimes fundamentally, on these matters; yet it might be suggested that, to the extent that it has an effect, the African experience - as seen by Black South Africans - has for the most part had a sobering, even conservative, impact.

A FUTURE REGIONAL AND FOREIGN POLICY

a) A SOUTHERN AFRICAN REGIONAL POLICY

In response to the question of how they saw a post-apartheid South Africa's relationship with the countries of the southern African region, a very strong desire for close and constructive relationships was expressed by all. Answers were all very positive and optimistic about the future. Part of the optimism arose from the belief that most intra-regional problems were caused by the White racist Government and these would disappear automatically once majority rule was achieved. More than one person made the point that there could be no solution to any of the problems of Lesotho, Swaziland and Botswana without a solution to the South African problem, and that Zimbabwe, Mozambique, Zambia, Angola and even Tanzania would not be able to deal satisfactorily with their political, economic and social difficulties until apartheid was ended. The group were all confident that cooperation would follow easily and that South Africa had the capacity to contribute economically to the growth of the region. The following comment, by a woman associated with trade unions, was representative of the feeling of goodwill:

> Once we've settled our problems we should not be selfish with other countries who are not wealthy, and we should not bully them. We should accommodate them and work hand in hand with them as sisters and brothers and as neighboring countries. They have contributed a lot to South African wealth, particularly their labor, and therefore they must be given an amount of recognition and respect.

Acknowledgement of the role of southern African workers in building South Africa was made by a number of speakers. Also acknowledged was the contribution of some of the neighboring states (and the suffering they incurred as a result) to the struggle to liberate South Africa. A businessman explained with enthusiasm:

> Nkrumah's theory will come into play. There will be a federation from Zambia downward. That is my dream. There will be a huge mineral and resource base. It will be based on the US model. South Africa will be rich but sympathetic. We have fought alongside Frelimo, ZAPU, ZANU: they have all helped us. So we will be able to help them and thank them ... we will help people to liberate themselves from poor leadership; for example, Malawi.

Another businessman was even more enthusiastic:

> A Black government will eliminate the problem. Five years after that there will be a Southern African Economic Community like the E.E.C. and twenty years later a common country with one capital. We will respect the sovereignty of all, even of Banda, but he will turn. A free South Africa will play a role as engine of the subcontinent. We owe them something. They helped us a lot.

There is, of course, contained within these two quotes, a potentially serious difference of opinion. This relates to whether South Africa would deal with all regional states irrespective of ideological leanings and assistance given to their own liberation struggle, or whether it would be selective in its alliances, and even possibly consider intervention to bring down what it might see as reactionary regimes: Banda's name cropped up most frequently in this regard. It will be recalled that he was the most disliked African leader still in power. This question was raised by a young educationist in the Eastern Cape:

> We will give support economically, and in all ways to help small dependent countries. We will help them end Savimbi and MNR [the anti-Frelimo movement in Mozambique]. We will aid them because they are so dependent now. I don't know how it will be but some people support the winds of change blowing back across Africa. We would help oust Banda in other words. Some would let South Africa become an imperialist power in Africa; others would not want this to happen; others would want to help bring about change in southern Africa.

The reference to the "winds of change blowing back" across Africa is an interesting one. It refers to British Prime Minister Harold Macmillan's warning to South Africa that in the 1960s the winds of change, which referred to the rise of African nationalism and the consequent political independence of African countries, would blow south across the continent and would soon reach South Africa. The notion that in a post-revolutionary situation, South Africa might play an effective role in undermining neo-colonialism and imperialism is one which some African academics and opposition politicians, disappointed in the performance of their own states, may well be talking about. It was not, however, one to which most of those interviewed for this Study would take seriously. A noninterventionist approach (including nonintervention in Malawi) was favored by the large majority. In the words of an academic councillor, "liberating" Africans countries "is not our business. This is a matter of internal cleansing." A lawyer agreed: "A policy of nonintervention of course. Even Banda, poor Banda, let him be."

A number of speakers referred to the fact that South Africa would remain the economic giant of the region and would need to be sensitive to the needs and demands of smaller countries. A young Durban man, with trade union affiliations, warned that, in trying to give constructive assistance to its neighbors, care would have to be taken to ensure that the assistance was determined by the people of those countries: "We must not say this is what we want to give you, for example, on technology. We must not promote our technology. That's what the US and the Soviet Union do." Yet while taking care not to dominate, it had, according to an Azapo supporter, to do enough to ensure that imperialism be kept at bay. It must be pragmatic, he said, but pragmatism "requires anti-capitalism and the destruction of imperialism."

This optimism about a post-apartheid South Africa's capacity to assist the region may be misplaced. It will be confronted by widespread poverty, large-scale unemployment and an economy that will probably be in very serious trouble. It will be sorely tested to feed all of its own people, provide health facilities, education and respond to formidable land and labor demands. Yet only one person introduced a note of warning about the limits on South Africa's future assistance. She said: "South Africa will be a bleeding country. It will need to build itself. For at least the first five or ten years we will be finding our own feet."

Only one of the group, a Nactu-affiliated trade union official, referred specifically to building a relationship with the Southern African Development Coordinating Council (SADCC). He thought that the best way to ensure that a new South Africa was not an "imperialist animal" and to help neighboring countries realize their potential was an early entry into, and an endorsement of the principles of, SADCC. He also argued that there should then be a reduction of foreign aid to SADCC and an increase in assistance from South Africa. "We should work towards a community which is interlinked and interdependent and maximizes the potential of the region. This could be done across ideological lines."

Given the central importance of race in the South African conflict (as discussed in the Introduction, racial categorization has been at the core of apartheid's oppressive legislation, and race presents itself as the obvious and immediate mobilizing factor in the struggle) the growing concern among more politicized Black South Africans - so clear from earlier chapters- with economic exploitation, class oppression and with socialist alternatives is a significant development with important potential influence on the region. For, in ideological terms, southern Africa is rather finely balanced. Angola and Mozambique represent the most left-leaning of these states. Tanzania (not in southern Africa, but a member of SADCC and bound to be of relevance) and Zimbabwe would come next. Moving further along a left-right continuum we would find Zambia and then Botswana, Swaziland, Lesotho and Malawi. The most significant of these states are inclined towards socialism. Yet given the difficulties of Mozambique and Angola (both seriously exacerbated by South African interventions), and Tanzania, the strength of the capitalist sector in Zimbabwe, and the prevailing influence of Western interests in the area, capitalism would still appear to be the predominant force in the region. Therefore, a socialist post-apartheid South Africa could make a profound impact on the evolving social and economic structure of the whole region. In world power terms, the stakes in the conflict would therefore become much higher. As an academic noted:

> It is about the world spheres of influence. In the long run in the southern African situation, it is a struggle for the control of capital, of the means of production, between two social systems, and the Reagan administration sees it in that light. Changes here will threaten to cause social upheaval in neighboring countries and affect the East-West relations. The US wants to keep the region in the fort. International capital knows that there must be change- else there is a threat of great fundamental change beyond South Africa's borders. So Western Governments want to broaden the social base of the South African Government

but this is to stem the tide of possible fundamental social change.

b) A FUTURE FOREIGN POLICY

QUESTION: In a future post-apartheid South Africa, what foreign policy would you like to see pursued?

Non-aligned - 51 (64% of those who expressed an opinion); Pro-West - 9; Pro-East - 5; Non-aligned with a Pro-Western tendency - 4; Non-aligned with an Pro-Eastern tendency - 9; Conditional - 2; Don't know - 2.

In response to this question, non-alignment - "down the center" - was by far the most broadly accepted direction. A point made by a number of them was that while they acknowledged the assistance of the Soviet Union in the liberation struggle, they did not believe they should therefore be permanently indebted to that country and they were determined to chart an independent course. One man warned that if the Soviet Union was helping as an "investment" in South Africa's future foreign policy, this was unacceptable. If it was identifying itself with the struggle without strings it was acceptable and would lead to good, but not subservient, ties. A couple of other people commented that in very practical terms they were worried about the apparent incapacity of the Soviet Union to give substantial assistance in peaceful situations. Mozambique's economic woes and vulnerability to pressure by Pretoria was seen as just such an example of Soviet capacity to help with armed struggle, but not with economic development. Only one person, himself anti-Western, questioned the quality of Soviet military assistance in southern Africa:

> Surely it is so powerful that it could give the kind of help that would bring down this Government. Why aren't people trained in the Soviet Union more effective? Some people die in situations which look like poor training. Why are the Front Line States so vulnerable to South Africa? If the Soviet Union really wanted to make South Africa more vulnerable why doesn't it install effective Soviet missiles? It could protect their borders and South African planes would not cross over. They could be dealt with. The Soviets are not pulling all their weight.

The arguments for a non-aligned position varied. One saw foreign policy as an extension of domestic policy, and that a balanced or mixed internal system would be reflected in an international relations posture. "We should go the Mugabe route, that is a neo-capitalist/socialist stew. We should take from the East and from the West." In fact a few people answered the question as though it were really about domestic policies. A second point was that both sides were technologically advanced and a future South Africa would have much to learn and gain from both:

> America has the capacity to produce the atom bomb. So do the Russians. Then both are capable of producing energy in various forms. I'm not able to say that either of these two systems lacks productive capacity. So we don't need to enter the dispute.

A third line of argument was that non-alignment was a component part of autonomy and the end of subservience.

> Independence is a better word than non-alignment. The Soviet Union and the US will be able to influence us but we will not be totally subservient. Obviously alignments will be there and will continue. But we are aware of this and afraid of becoming puppets.

An extension of this argument was the need to be free to make decisions one way or the other on their merits. Fourthly, there was the view that a future South Africa would be best off working closely with Africa and the third world and therefore it would do well to become a part of the non-aligned movement.

> I take refuge in a non-aligned position. But it has to be of a kind which will be of assistance to other countries to help them to become independent of Eastern and Western hegemony, and will be supportive of other non-aligned countries. Mugabe's position this weekend [at the Non-Aligned Conference in Harare] was important, and his cooperation with [Prime Minister] Gandhi. We must chart a pragmatic non-aligned course to give sustenance to those who wish to be non-aligned and throw off domination.

Then there were the more clearly economic reasons. Some of these were put forward by people who were extremely angry with the US and the West, yet felt that it would be necessary to retain a working relationship with the West. One man related this to the need he felt there was bound to be for development assistance from the West to help deal with the severe problems of poverty which would be apartheid's legacy. A Nactu-affiliated union official explained:

> Initially the people will be more pro-East, but that will depend to some extent on how protracted the struggle will be. But after the honeymoon is over, people will assess more realistically their reliance on first world economies. I personally don't have a preference. We must avoid the mistakes of Machel - if you want tractors, get tractors, don't accept tanks. In Zimbabwe a trade union received a dismantled asbestos trade union center, but the people forgot to send money to erect it. So the equipment is there but it has not been constructed. We must be able to negotiate what we want.

A graduate student, socialist in orientation, agreed with this line of argument:

> Where do we start? We are part of the world market. We definitely need to interact with other countries, East and West, for our survival. The basis of our economy is export-oriented. We can't survive without Western interaction and trading. Socialism doesn't mean that you become so dogmatic that you say that our foreign policy will look only to the USSR.

Another line of reasoning mentioned by only one person (a senior UDF sympathizer with diplomatic concerns) was that at this particular stage of the struggle Black people needed all the world support they could get and therefore it was important to stress non-alignment.

Others seemed to select non-alignment because they were not comfortable with either of the great powers and in a sense they had yet to think the topic through to a satisfactory solution. This is one example:

> I select non-alignment, like the rest of Africa. We must still choose sides on different issues. I am not a supporter of the Soviet Union, but will feel no difficulty in joining with them for purposes of the struggle. I have my own qualms about what they do. Some of the Western Governments have improved their policies. But America is all over, interfering in Nicaragua, Vietnam, Angola. When we are all free, we will meet in solidarity and America will be in danger. Also, here we will look at the scars left by the police and military using American equipment.

Amongst those who wished to take sides there was more sympathy in this group for a pro-Western rather than a pro-Eastern posture. The strongest statement came from a priest:

> It should definitely not be East-leaning. I despise Communism. I've not visited a Communist country but I have spoken to people from Communist countries and they say they have a great deal of repression. We don't know them. They can give us arms for war, etc., but nothing else. They won't be able to help us in the long term. So we don't owe them anything. So we should definitely not be pro-East. Also, we will have to deal with the West because their companies will still be here, the US, UK, Japan and others, and we will want them to be here. It is a dream to think that we will take over all corporations. So we will have to be pro-West. But we must control this closely so that companies do not exploit us and they leave some reasonable profits here. Neutrality or non-alignment is not a reality. We need to relate to the West and get what we can get out of the relationship.

A number of people made the point that they felt more at ease with the West because they were more familiar with it. One man who generally favored non-alignment acknowledged that "maybe because of brainwashing I feel more comfortable with the West." Another man, also in general fairly sympathetic to non-alignment said nevertheless that "those of us who were educated in the West prefer a Western inclination." And yet another person seemed to be pointing to habit: "this type of Western economic, political and social life has been drilled into us. We don't want now to start a new type of economic system." By contrast, people noted how little they knew of the Soviet system: "We know nothing much about Russia. We know they are a friend. But we don't know their system."

The difficulties which would be confronted in pursuing a pro-Eastern policy were acknowledged by those who supported such a policy. Not only would long-established economic and cultural ties have to be disrupted but people would need to be socialized to accept this.

> A pro-Eastern policy will be more beneficial to us. But we must not adopt everything entirely. It will be very difficult because everybody will have to be re-educated. We used to be communalistic, but now because of outside influence we are so deeply capitalistic.

A few people commented that pro-Eastern sympathy was increasing among the young and the trade unions. Most support in this group of interviewees did come from students, but not the majority of them; but trade unionists seemed to favor non-alignment. Also the BC view on a pro-Eastern policy was that this should be directed toward African socialist states, Cuba and China, and not the Soviet Union.

There were some other points which were of interest. One was that this decision will need to made on the basis of the best interests of the people at the time and would therefore need to be left open now and decided upon at the appropriate time "by the people for the people. It was not up to politicians and intellectuals alone to determine this, nor to do so in advance."

The question of people's influence on foreign relations is difficult in any circumstances. Something of the problem can be seen in the following statement by an activist shop steward, a person working at a lower hierarchical level and with a lower level of education than most of the group.

> On foreign policy I can't tell you straight. The Russians are trying to influence us. They want to come here. I can't tell if we want them here or not. I don't know clearly what terrorists are. I hear always about the Russians as terrorists. In SASOL [a South African parastatal for which the interviewee had worked] the White manager always told us that the Russians wanted this country. Some people say the unions are communist.

Another view was that it would depend on the behavior of the great powers during the liberation struggle. This referred particularly to the US, since Soviet support was clear.

> It depends on how freedom comes. If America will do its bit to help us, we will be pro-West. If not, then we will be pro-East. Nothing for nothing and very little for sixpence.

And:

> We call on all people to help us. In the process Thatcher and the others will in effect spell out our future international relations. It is non-aligned at the moment. But it may not remain so. Kohl and the others may think they are safeguarding German interests and employment. But in the long term their support for Pretoria will jeopardize their interests in this country. Young people and others are turning to the East.

Attitudes at this stage did not amount to a future foreign policy. Yet the strong preference for a non-aligned policy was significant, given the broad and deep anger expressed towards the US and the substantial support given the liberation movement by the Soviet Union and the Eastern bloc, which most people genuinely appreciated.

This appears to be the one area where the South African media and censorship on literature and control of political material and passports seems to have worked. On most other issues, for example Libya and Afghanistan, people reacted almost automatically against this. Here they did not. They were aware of a bias in the media and of the fact that they had been kept in ignorance of the Soviet Union and they acknowledged their ignorance. Clearly too Western culture, education, media etc. to which they have been long accustomed have made some of them feel more comfortable with the West. This of course may not be true of exiles, and may be less true of younger persons. Trade unions seemed to have been affected to some extent by their current assessment of worker freedom in the Eastern bloc, particularly as illustrated by the Solidarity example.

So a notable increase in anti-capitalism and in socialism has not translated into a wish for a pro-Eastern foreign policy. It has resulted in a strong plea for non-alignment and a determination to judge international issues on their merits. This may, of course, change over time, and it will be affected by the progress of the struggle and the way in which the US responds to the situation in South Africa.

1986/87 - A NEW AMERICAN POLICY

Between the two rounds of interviews four noteworthy events occurred which related to US-South African relations. These were the Sanctions Act passed by Congress, the acceleration in the pace of American companies disinvesting, the meeting between the US Secretary of State George Shultz and the President of the ANC, Oliver Tambo, and the appointment for the first time of a Black American Ambassador to Pretoria. Because of the legislative restrictions included in the state of emergency - mentioned in the Introduction - it was decided in 1986 not to ask direct questions about sanctions and disinvestment. It was nevertheless abundantly clear from the responses that most of those interviewed were in favor of both. President Reagan's opposition to these steps was without doubt a major cause of their feeling of hostility toward him and his Administration. So too was the US failure to have any high level official contact with the ANC. I discussed the possibility of the appointment of a Black Ambassador with only a few people; they were all opposed to the idea.

On the surface at least the US had therefore appeared to have complied to some extent with these demands. For purposes of evaluating attitudes these steps by the US were helpful. Not only were the responses to each of these important in themselves but their combined impact on Black perceptions of the US - in simple terms, did it cause people to change their minds? - helps us to understand what is a major quest in this Study, namely how deep the sense of antagonism ran and how solid was its basis. In this chapter we will deal with the four policy changes. The assessment of their impact will be included in the following concluding chapter.

a) THE SANCTIONS ACT OF OCTOBER 1986

In October 1986, overriding the veto of the President, the US Congress passed the "Comprehensive Anti-Apartheid Act of 1986." This included the following prohibitive provisions: importation of Krugerrands, military articles, products originating from South African parastatals, agricultural and food products, iron and steel, and sugar; and loans to the South African Government, new investment in South Africa, US Government procurement from South Africa, promotion of US tourism to South Africa, US Government involvement in trade with South Africa, sale of items on the munitions list, cooperation with the South African Armed forces and export of petroleum products. (See Public Law 99-440. An Act to Prohibit Loans to, other Investment in, and Certain other Activities with respect to South Africa, and for other Purposes.) The Act also contained provisions for further intensifying sanctions, and for taking measures against countries which might take advantage of the US sanctions for their own benefit (see sections 402 and 508).

Despite the title of the legislation, this was clearly not a comprehensive set of sanctions. As a letter from thirty-three members of the US House of Representatives pointed out a year after the enactment of these provisions, the "sanctions are 'relatively weak and contain several loopholes' affecting only one-third of US imports from South Africa and 'virtually no exports,' nor had the administration implemented some of the provisions required by law."[1] Evidence would suggest that the Reagan Administration went to considerable trouble to undermine the impact of the legislation in practice.[2] Nevertheless, the Act did go considerably further than anything previously decreed against South Africa, and was seen at the time in the US as forcing some alteration of policy on an unwilling President.

Given the restrictions imposed by South African law it was felt that it would be inappropriate to ask interviewees to deal with this question on a personal approval/disapproval basis. They were therefore asked whether they thought sanctions had any impact, material, psychological or otherwise, and whether they thought Black South Africans had been pleased by the passing of the Act.[*] For purposes of the study I wished to maintain a distinction between the Sanctions Act and the process of disinvestment. It became clear early on that most of the interviewees were not differentiating between the two. After their introductory remarks indicated that they were talking about both, they were asked to distinguish between them and to talk about sanctions first. Although they took note of this request, I did not feel that in all cases they were making a clear distinction. One man, an opponent of both, said that he saw them as one and the same thing since their consequences would be the same.

A second observation about the responses on sanctions was that a large proportion of the group were not familiar with the contents of the Act. Most of those who were specifically asked about this admitted that they did not know much detail about the Act and they did not think that most others did. A university research associate said: "People are pleased with anything anti-South African. If it puts South Africa on trial, good. But people are not familiar with the details. Even I am not familiar with the details and I am a researcher."

The explanations given for this apparent lack of attention to an initiative which the previous year had been seen as potentially so important were varied. One interpretation (mentioned by a few people) related to the coinciding of the passing of the Act with a moment of great pressure on Black South Africans.

> When it was passed people were caught up in local issues, the state of emergency, detentions. They had no time to reflect on this. It came at the wrong psychological moment. A lot of the political leadership was in detention. The opposition forces were in disarray and local stuff took preeminence in people's minds. Also the results are not immediately tangible. Maybe in five years time we'll see the results. Blacks here seem more pleased that Reagan was under pressure than with the Bill itself. Suddenly he faced a test of credibility, and this could lead to a change in American policies.

Also, because of the state of emergency, Black organizations were not allowed to call meetings to inform their followers of the contents of the legislation. People had come to rely on their organizations for the dissemination of this kind of information. Sanctions came at a time of severe official restriction on Black political communication; there was little opportunity to explain or to hold open discussion. A few people commented that their lack of knowledge resulted from their having been in prison at the time of enactment and for a further eight or nine months thereafter. Yet others argued that they themselves, as well as people they knew, did not take the contents seriously because of a deeply felt mistrust of, and cynicism about, American actions in South Africa.

This last point was confirmed by the fact that one of the most common responses - mentioned more than 30 times- expressed some form of suspicion about the motives lying behind the Act. As can be seen from the quotes that follow, the sources of suspicion and the bases of disappointment vary. If there was a central theme to be derived from the answers it lay in a deep mistrust of the US built up over the previous ten years or so. Other comments varied from charges that the sanctions were too weak and implementation was ineffective, to arguments that any gains had already been eroded by intensified pressure and that sanctions were more an "American football" than a method of liberation, and to the acknowledgement that there may have been exaggerated expectations of what sanctions could achieve.

Suspicion of American motives were expressed by a number of people. A middle-aged woman from the Eastern Cape maintained that "even a vote of Congress we can't believe. We want to discover what the trick is." A young university lecturer said:

> Anti-Americanism is so deeply felt. America would not do anything that is not in America's interest. Also this was an election year in America and this decision was part of that process.

An organizer of a trade union support group commented:

> Americans don't need these things. They have got enough steel and coal. They have excluded the stuff they need. This kind of partial sanctions can't be effective. Even on the items they are embargoing they don't have a monopoly on the market.

An official of a trade union affiliated to Cosatu said:

> The Black worker is very suspicious of the sincerity of American policy. What is passed in America and what is implemented are very different things. We also know that sanctions are very difficult to police firmly.... The West has a tendency to go public in terms of propaganda on

> these decisions ... still it was welcomed by the working class ... only afterwards they learnt it was meaningless.

An Azapo supporter added:

> We support sanctions. But when America called for it I was surprised. What motive could they have? The genuineness of their commitment to our struggle is questionable. It is contradicted by US operations in southern Africa, especially in Angola, and by its arrogance in calling on the Front Line States to renounce support for violence - as if they were the only people to support violence - or else they won't get aid.

A number of people were dubious about American sincerity in implementing the sanctions, suggesting for example that there was "a lot of ducking by the US Government" and "behind-the-door dealings going on." A trade unionist in Cape Town referred to the problem of inflated hopes:

> There was a basic expectation among a section of the people that it would hasten the downfall of the State. When that did not happen this led to a surge of disappointment and then to very strong criticism. It had no material impact.

His own union, he added, had anticipated that accompanying the sanctions would be increased aid from US sources to assist Black organizations to initiate community projects to help respond to the increased suffering that would result.

An almost equal number of comments indicated a positive response to the passing of the Act. Some of these respondents went on to say that they later became disillusioned because of the apparent lack of impact or of implementation. A young lawyer explained:

> Anything that will hurt this Government will be welcome. People still want it ... although they still blame America for acting too late.

Along the same lines a journalist observed:

> People are rejoicing to see tensions build up between Pretoria and Washington. People rejoice when they see the South African Government lose friends. America, being one of the biggest allies of South Africa, one has watched the fiery exchange and hostile attitudes developing from Pretoria and Washington.

He went on to explain that for a variety of reasons - mainly that sanctions were not producing results - local issues had become more pressing and relevant. An Azapo official said that it had been a step in the right direction, but that lack of coordination with Western Governments would render it ineffective. A professional man in Durban, while acknowledging that no material impact was discernible, nevertheless felt that it was seen as a "positive signal" to progressives in South Africa. It had also introduced South Africans to the complexities of American politics, to the differences between the Administration, the Congress and the people. He saw it as a victory for the US Anti-Apartheid Movement in the teeth of opposition from the President. He had recently visited the US and consequently had come to appreciate this; "Nine out of ten [Black South Africans] would not know the extent of that victory." The only other person in the group who gave this kind of answer had also paid a recent visit to America. Two others who were positive about the passing of the Act based their satisfaction on the defeat of Reagan, rather than on the Act's direct significance for South Africa.

Assessments of the impact on South Africa of the sanctions may be divided into four main types: no impact; a negative impact on Blacks; a negative impact on Whites; and an inability to assess.

The most common response (mentioned 34 times) was that it had had no or very little impact. (10 said no effect; 4- very little impact; 4 - no effect on the South African Government; 8 - no economic effect; 4 - very little economic effect; 3

- it could not bring the Government down; and 3 - the Government had prepared in advance and therefore it could have no impact.) A professional-level manager said that South Africa had stockpiled strategic supplies in advance, and observed further that the South African economy had long been structured in response to political and ideological demands rather than market forces, and therefore it would be able to adapt to the new pressures. A researcher said that South Africa had done its "homework" and was ready; and a community organizer commented:

> The South African Government is very strong. Unemployment was very high anyway. It has made very little difference to our suffering. It affected the Government on a very low scale. People were pleased because they thought the Government was not as strong as it is. We have learnt quickly.

As regards impact on the Black population, a senior-level manager stated:

> Black people accept it. The Black man is hungry whether he is working or not working. When he gets sacked we are sorry, but his brothers and sisters will help. Nobody is going to die. We will help.

Twenty of the responses included comments to the effect that Black people had suffered as a consequence of sanctions. (13 said that it had caused unemployment; 5 that it had worsened working conditions; and 2 that Black people were not pleased by its effects.) The interviewees that were most convinced that it was having a deleterious effect on Blacks were primarily people who were opposed to it in the first place. A manager working with a private foundation concluded:

> I am opposed to it. People were put out of work and it has not changed the Government. The Black leadership is concerned about sanctions, but our people are not. They want food and shelter.

An Inkatha organizer was also critical:

> It is having effects. But the effects it is having are not the ones intended. It has hurt Blacks more than Whites. Next door is the manpower building dealing with unemployment. People in large numbers are lining up outside. Sanctions helped Whites to rally round the Government-they felt threatened and became more conservative. This was reflected in the election. The Progressive Federal Party was washed away and the Conservative Party became the official opposition. The National Party won an outstanding majority. And South African troops are hitting neighboring countries. Black people are still detained in large numbers. People in the forefront [of Black politics] are thinking twice about this. People are not pleased. And the social programs of these companies are ended or reduced.

A second Inkatha supporter, a woman, said that a small group had been affected and they were angry. "People," she argued, "will lose jobs, go hungry and die." A technical assistant, an ANC sympathizer, acknowledged that it did weigh heavily on some people who had lost jobs.

> I know too many people who have lost jobs. But if people say they are disappointed about losing jobs that does not mean that they want to go on being oppressed.

Fifteen comments referred to some negative effects on Whites and/or the Government. (6 said that it had threatened the Government in some way; 5 that it had affected the economy negatively; 3 that Whites had suffered; and 1 that Whites had suffered psychologically.) "The Government did panic," said one middle-aged woman. A graduate student agreed:

> Government felt threatened. It knows the consequences of sanctions, and the power of sanctions in arousing militancy and revolutionary instincts on the part of the exploited and unemployed, and that it breeds anger.

A university researcher commented:

> It has had an effect on the economy. It has actually stalled quite a few things. There is a lot of uncertainty about the continuation of American companies and on projected investment.

A community activist in Cape Town said:

> I am very happy the bill was passed. It has had effects. Thousands of people have lost jobs, not only Blacks, but also Whites, and certain White firms have gone bankrupt.

A worker superviser in a private organization added:

> I have to mix sanctions and disinvestment. People are pleased with both. In the short term it will harm Blacks but in the long term it will bring liberation. White people will also suffer because firms will close down. If I lose my job I will be pleased because the White man will also be in trouble; because I will become a criminal and deal with the White man directly. Whenever he is at work he will have to employ a guard at home and so will have to pay for it. He will realize that he is forced to do all this because of Government policy.

By contrast, four people made the point that the major impact of sanctions on Whites was to mobilize and unify them. "It mobilized [them] in order to overcome it. It sent Whites back into the laager and caused more hatred."

It was clear from most of the comments that concrete and conclusive evidence on the effects of sanctions was in short supply. Ten answers specifically included this point: it was "too soon" or "too early" to be able to assess the effects; "no data were available;" "there was an economic recession unrelated to sanctions;" "open debate on this is restricted;" and "the Government and the White media control the facts." In a recent article, Minter has commented on the complexity of disentangling the various political effects of sanctions and determining economic projections:

> Analysts tend to underestimate the effects of sanctions by concentrating on symbolic short-term rather than substantive long-term consequences and by stressing the isolated effects of single measures rather than the cumulative impact and the interaction of sanctions with other factors influencing economic and political confidence.

"In the short run," he continues, "sanctions are likely to produce defiance [on the part of Whites] rather than surrender."[3]

Certainly at the time the interviews were undertaken, analyzing short- and long-term impacts and distinguishing between different causes of specific consequences remained very problematic.

b) DISINVESTMENT BY US FIRMS

In 1984, 7 US companies pulled out of South Africa; in 1985, this rose to 40, in 1986, to 50, and in the first half of 1987 (at which stage the second round of research was undertaken), 33 more companies left. This brought the total number of companies which had disinvested to 130, and indicated an accelerating trend.[4] Both because of legal restrictions and because of the complexity of the topic, the question put to the group was not framed on an approval/disapproval basis. Interviewees were requested to structure their answers around the questions of whether they considered the disinvestments were having any impact of any kind and whether they felt Black people were pleased by the companies departing. Answers, quite appropriately, were multifaceted and therefore difficult to classify and quantify.

By far the most common response (mentioned 35 times) was that the processes involved did not amount to disinvestment. 18 comments, many made in conjunction with the first point, claimed that disinvestment had had no effect, political or economic. 20 responses, by contrast, stated that Blacks had suffered as a consequence. 10 said they thought Black people were pleased and 10 disagreed. 10 argued either for more careful targeting of sectors, or for a different form of disinvestment more advantageous to workers, and 6 people said that Cosatu and other leaders were rethinking the whole issue.

The dominant point made was that the companies which had announced that they were withdrawing were not in reality disinvesting. What would have satisfied the definition of real disinvestment was not made clear. Based on my understanding of discussions in 1986, it was generally anticipated that disinvestment would amount to a closing down of facilities and a complete withdrawal of the companies, together with their products, their technology and their expertise. Unavoidably, this would cause hardship for Black people who would be unemployed, but Whites would also suffer and it was necessary to put pressure on the South African economy and on the Government. With the exception of Kodak (which many people confirmed had withdrawn in a real sense), most companies had not done this, leading to considerable cynicism and doubt about the intentions and sincerity of these companies. What then was actually happening, and how did the interviewees interpret the process? First, a senior manager (strongly pro-private enterprise) with a firm in the Eastern Cape explained:

> It amounts to a management buy-out. General Motors becomes Delta Motors, and the current White managers are put in a position where they can purchase the company outright. Young people, Afrikaners, could not have bought the companies in their individual capacity. The South African Government has become involved in assisting them. Volkskas Bank has risen to prominence as a merchant bank - from being a small savings bank for the Afrikaans community. So the Government, through Volkskas, helped these people to buy these companies. Immediately the new owners could make bold statements that they would renew contracts with the South African Government and Defence Force - US companies could not do that - and they were not bothered with the response of Black trade unions to that. In addition, those corporations that left did so for economic reasons, not political ones. They were not profitable any more, partly because wages are not as low as they used to be.

He proceeded to give an example of Ford which, he said, had built a recreation center for Black workers "to gain Brownie points under the Sullivan Code." When the company left, it reneged on its commitment to its Black workers by allowing these facilities to pass into White hands. An academic who worked with Cosatu-affiliated trade unions and supported disinvestment saw it in these terms:

> People feel there is no disinvestment. Ford became something else; but surely if you look at the shareholders and the dividends paid the names won't have changed. It is not really disinvestment. It is a complex question. There is no pure American capital operating in any one company. Possibly they have a majority of shares but there will also be some South African and British interests. It's always mixed. So pulling out means that you transfer to another party already in that corporation some more shares and you give them a loan to buy your investment and so ensure that your investment remains secure. It cannot close down. Capital will not close down.... We want real disinvestment because business strengthens the State, for example, by paying taxes to the Government.

According to an Azapo supporter:

> When we investigate these actions we see a perpetuation of control by one superior race over another. It is just a change of masters.... They are indigenizing oppression. Now Afrikaners will be more cruel because they are not responsible to international public opinion. Azapo is for total disinvestment. People should pack up and leave the country because we are in a campaign to isolate South Africa. We are not interested in selective or conditional disinvestment.

A businessman who had gone to considerable length to find ways for Black businessmen to take over some of these companies' interests agreed, despite a very different approach to the topic:

> We are seeing management buy-outs which have not included Blacks. Top White guys in management have become instant millionaires, and Blacks remain sloggers as before. It is racism. The White people who take over are not putting their own money into it. We tried to take over Coca Cola. Financial institutions, banks, here and in the US refused us. They opened their checkbooks and signed for Whites, but not for Blacks. So far there is no unemployment because it is all a trick. Kodak is the only exception.

A young woman UDF supporter in Natal questioned:

> Are they actually leaving? Or just staying in another name? It does have some minimal impact in terms of good propaganda for these companies and the US Government. There is no extra unemployment. The reputation of the US is so bad that we always look below the surface. They are trying to please us but they are not sincere. The way it is happening adds to our doubts. And some companies are staying. It should be done more honestly.

In agreeing with the above comments a man who worked for the UDF added that the South African forces calling for disinvestment now found that they had lost control of the process and had become alarmed at the way in which it was being handled.

> Our view is that the transfer of ownership is not ending American involvement in South Africa. There is a minimum degree of upset for the ruling class, but it still has access to the products and the technology. Disinvestment has been worked out with the local ruling class and we have lost control. Now they are opening up the share markets to Blacks. One company is placing shares in trust so that employees can buy up the shares over time. This is positive in the sense of creating involvement of the indigenous middle class, but at the same time it is undermining and dividing some of the forces of the opposition. They have opposed the State's attempts to create and coopt a Black middle class; so now disinvesting companies are trying to do the same thing. So the trade unions want consultation on this before companies leave. We don't know what the new parameters are going to be.

The notion that this selling to White management amounted to a public relations trick - "They are not withdrawing. They are not disappearing. Their products go on being made." - was widely accepted. Further, there was a feeling, that to the extent that they acted at all, these corporations were responding to economic realities at home and/or in South Africa, rather than in support of Black liberation. A BC-oriented trade unionist saw disinvestment as mainly motivated by the parent companies' predicament in the US. He used the Kodak case as an example. According to this informant, Kodak had tendered for three major contracts in New York State. They had been warned that if there were "any hassle factors" caused by their South African interests they would lose the contracts. It was therefore a business decision to go home. So too, according to this same man, was General Motors' decision.

The next most frequently mentioned comment was that Black people had suffered as a result of the disinvestments. A senior executive with a private foundation explained:

> There has not been much affect on the economy. At the same time as the companies are being taken over by South African private enterprise, Black workers are not enjoying the same privileges as before. Workers are also unhappy about not being informed in good time of the withdrawal. Now there is a cry: Why do you leave us? People are scared of losing the privileges they had under the Sullivan Code.

A woman in a private company asked:

> Who will be the worst sufferers from disinvestment? We Blacks will. Look at the number of companies that have pulled out. Blacks have become angrier in the last year. They are opposed to disinvestment.

A UWUSA trade unionist closely associated with Inkatha in Natal agreed that people were losing jobs. He felt that, as a result, crime and bank robberies were increasing, that people were becoming more desperate and less humane and this was leading to social "malaise." An Inkatha official also saw the results as negative. He gave as an example his own brother, a father of many children, who had lost a job. "This is why people are becoming hoboes." The only person who attempted to present some kind of statistical evidence on this topic was a trade unionist who supported disinvestment. He felt that the results had not been significant. "Possibly 3000 workers have lost jobs as a result compared to 3 million unemployed in total."

Ten responses included comments claiming that Black South Africans were pleased by announcements of disinvestment. A woman student in Cape Town, while acknowledging that there did not seem to be much change, said that Blacks were very pleased to see anything that helped end apartheid. A legal adviser explained her sense of satisfaction in this way:

> Suffering has not increased because of disinvestment. The companies which are leaving are the same ones which did not pay a living wage and exploited Black workers. If they had paid a living wage we would welcome them to stay. Blacks were not better off when they were here. We are very happy when they go. People are pleased because they see the pressure building up.

Interviewees who argued that Blacks were positive, also asserted that disinvestments were having an impact on Whites. A trade union organizer said that it had made a psychological impact on the Government, which had led to strong anti-American feeling in Pretoria. A graduate student argued that when Barclays Bank announced that it was disinvesting, many Afrikaners woke up to the fact that in the 1980s things had changed.

> It has thrown Afrikaners out of their cocoons and at least made them aware. It has helped shake many people out of their complacency. Blacks don't want disinvestment but it is the only strategy that will work - so they do want it. But not total disinvestment - there is a change in tone from last year.

A trade unionist affiliated to Cosatu felt that it had created uncertainty among Whites and that this could be seen in the number of Whites, particularly professionals, taking the "chicken run," that is, emigrating. About ten comments supported the opposing view, namely that Blacks were not pleased by the disinvestment. There were also a number of people who admitted to mixed feelings about the experience so far. A university student said there had been different reactions:

> As much as people want disinvestment it has instilled fear when they face up to the stark facts of what it might mean. It has caused unemployment and this frightens people. The Government fears it also, but it is Black people who suffer. Whites are also being unemployed, but the Government won't admit it. We need to understand more about disinvestment. If I suffer, what do I gain? The short-term effect is what worries people.

An official working with an alternative education agency interpreted the effects in this way:

> It confuses the Pretoria Government. It makes us happy, just for a bit. Superficially happy but not deeply. The companies disinvest but research shows that they go on profiting and benefiting. There is now less emphasis on this among activists.

A lawyer employed by a legal advice bureau expressed concern:

> Obviously some people have lost jobs. It must affect them because there are no other jobs. My concern is that they are taking away our workers' efforts in the form of profits. We fear that capital created by workers is leaving the country. Those companies are only interested in profits, not workers. I am not sure about it being a victory. The fact that the Government is facing pressure in one form or another means that something is building up, although it hasn't yet helped the people affected.

And a priest in the Eastern Cape explained:

> It raises lots of problems. Workers have fears, but they also see that the Government fears disinvestment more than they do. Others feel a better option would have been to strengthen the military wing of the ANC. Most people in the democratic movement feel that the military option cannot be openly encouraged and therefore we are restricted to encouraging disinvestment ... but we have been discouraged by these companies simply being bought out.

Others made the argument that while leaders might be pleased the ordinary man or woman in the street was not; or that those who understood the objectives of the disinvestment campaign were pleased, while those that did not understand it could not be; or that there was a different response from those that had lost jobs from those that had not.

There was also a group of people who were of the opinion that Cosatu in particular, but also other leaders, were rethinking their strategy on disinvestment. A researcher in Durban explained the significance of this: "It all depends on Cosatu. People don't so much have their own opinions as they depend on significant actors, and they follow suit - Tutu, Mandela, Cosatu can say anything - and it is taken as correct." A manager argued that leaders who had earlier called for sanctions would not now openly admit their error because they would lose face. "I suspect though that there is less enthusiasm for it." An unaffiliated trade union organizer, who was of the opinion that the process was not operating to the advantage of the workers, agreed with this:

> Workers have been left in the lurch. People who were supposed to benefit have not benefited. Cosatu is saying it still, but they don't really believe it. They are not pushing it anymore. You will see this if you measure the follow-through in their interviews, publications, etc. There is a contradiction at the moment.... The image is there, but not the immediate follow-through.

An official of a union affiliated to Cosatu also agreed:

> People are rethinking and coming with ideas of how the campaign should be handled. We don't want money to go out of the country, or that we should lose jobs. This won't remove the Government, and putting people out of work is not going to solve the problem. ... What people would like to see happening, if possible, is to have companies pull out so as to leave a direct impact on the South African Government rather than affecting the employees only and immediately. For example, if access to technology could be limited it could cause problems for their projects, and the Government would be forced to do something. We are not looking for something dramatic like thousands losing jobs per day and then waiting to see if the Government will take notice. There is re-thinking about this in Cosatu: they want a more concrete approach than just a generalized support for anything that puts pressure.

A student explained what he saw as Cosatu's dilemma:

> They need to represent the workers, and if the people are not employed, then they don't represent them. The or-

> ganization becomes weaker. We need to say to the companies that if they want to stay, they should stay on our terms, and to our benefit.

A journalist added:

> There are effects but they are not very visible; and they are not seen or felt by the average man. Cosatu wants disinvestment to hit at the Government and not at the Black worker. We don't want to see American companies becoming spiteful by ensuring that when they leave they will cause large-scale suffering to make those who called for disinvestment suffer. There is a conscious effort by those companies to ensure that Blacks suffer. Cosatu is trying to stop this.

A graduate student saw the problem in this way:

> Trade unions are calling for an organization of the unemployed, because they have lost numbers. Most companies leaving were organized in unions. And so the unions are losing their membership, which affects the image of the trade unions. Disinvestment is not useful to the membership in this kind of crisis. It has weakened the unions by causing unemployment. They are aware that people are unemployed and that people are unhappy about that. The political people in the unions are still strongly in favor of disinvestment.

A middle-aged manager added:

> People are beginning to lose jobs. It is being debated now as workers continue to lose jobs. Cosatu may have to justify this to its workers. To the ordinary worker the importance of a union is to secure jobs and good wages.

These opinions came both from people who support and people who do not support Cosatu and disinvestment. An article in the sympathetic *Weekly Mail* entitled "Some gaps and some silences in Cosatu's disinvestment call" seemed to agree:

> The gaps are a mark of debates in progress and of questions which will have to be answered within the federation and its affiliates. Two of the major issues which will need clarifying are the share ownership issue and the practical demands which unions intend to make of companies planning to disinvest.[4]

In a press conference held immediately after the Cosatu national congress in July 1987 - in the middle of the second round of interviews for this Study - it was clear from the questions that the press too believed this. The Cosatu Executive appeared hesitant and discomfited by the questions, but stuck to its guns in its answers. A few excerpts from the press conference follow.

Question by a member of the press (q). Looking at your resolution on disinvestment there is no specific clause calling on companies to disinvest?

Answer by a member of the Cosatu executive (a). I think that this resolution needs to be read together with the resolution taken at last year's Congress, which has not been rescinded in any way. This resolution tries to deal with the concrete situation of companies pulling out as they like - and that there is no yardstick to measure what a good pull-out is and what a bad pull-out is.

q. Will Cosatu and its members be actively working to shut down companies that are operating in SA, or will you leave that for them to decide and then demand negotiation about how they leave?

a. Obviously our campaign will involve that as well. It will involve all forms of action to be decided by affiliates.

q. Will you from tomorrow or the next working day begin sending delegations from the various affiliates to visit companies to tell them to go, in the next twelve/ six/eighteen months and we want you to begin negotiating the pull out with us now?

a. We have taken a policy on disinvestment at our launching Congress as well. I think what has been applying up to now will continue. That aspect was not discussed.

q. At recent conferences with businessmen overseas the ANC has laid down certain things that companies can do apart from disinvesting, such as not paying national servicemen their salaries and embarking on certain types of social responsibility campaigns. Does Cosatu endorse that, does Cosatu have a set of guidelines to present to companies as alternatives to a pull-out. Has this been considered?

a. The direction that Cosatu takes is decided and shaped by the members themselves. So in each plant workers have to sit down and negotiate with management if it comes to that issue, and they will come out with what it is they are looking for, if they so decide that they want the company to disinvest Cosatu will back that call.

q. So Cosatu doesn't necessarily want all foreign companies to leave?

a. It does. There is a blanket call for disinvestment and sanctions.

And so on. Given that support for sanctions and disinvestment was and still is illegal and punishable in South Africa, and that the disinvestment experience was a very recent and still confusing one, and that corporate offers of some kind of Black participation had only just begun to be made, this was a remarkable and testing press conference. Hesitance of some kind would be more than understandable. Nevertheless, the tone of the answers seemed to indicate that at least a moment of re-assessment on disinvestment was taking place. It is however important not to prejudge the outcome of such re-thinking. And Cosatu has since stressed on a number of occasions that its policy remains unchanged.

The large majority of the group interviewed would have been in favor of disinvestment and sanctions the previous year. This was a key reason for the hostility felt towards the US then, particularly the Reagan Administration. Clearly, a good number of them - probably the majority - still did believe in this strategy. For these people, their ineffectiveness resulted from their very partial and insincere implementation. For them, then, strengthened and more comprehensive sanctions and complete disinvestment were required to have an impact on the Government. Another group would acknowledge the lack of effectiveness and seriousness of purpose of those withdrawing, and in consequence would be looking for more carefully targeted, maybe selective actions; ones that operated more directly against White interests and the Government and less immediately against Black people. Others again have become cynical that capital will ever respond substantively and positively to their struggle, and felt that other strategies needed to be stressed. Yet others feared that eventually capital might effectively withdraw, and their reading of even the minimal effects experienced so far frightened them into believing that growing numbers of Black workers would be unemployed and would in fact suffer seriously. The minority, primarily Inkatha members and some management personnel, opposed these measures from the start, and believed their arguments had proved to be well-founded. They claimed that Blacks were already suffering from these actions and would continue to do so as long as they were being implemented. Facts were in very short supply, and where and when available were, and seemed likely to remain, difficult to analyze. So at the time of the interviews perceptions were all important. It was very early to make assessments, and extremely problematic given the pressures brought to bear on Black leadership over the previous 24 months or so.

c) THE SHULTZ-TAMBO MEETING

The second half of 1986 also saw a meeting between the US Secretary of State, George Shultz, and the President of the ANC, Oliver Tambo, the first such official high level meeting between the US Administration and the ANC. The consistent refusal of the Reagan Administration to deal openly with the ANC and to recognize its significance for Black South Africans had been a further serious source of resentment among those interviewed in 1986. Interviewees were therefore asked in 1987

QUESTION: Did you approve of the meeting between Shultz and Tambo? Did you see it as a positive event, as meaningful to the Black cause?

Asked - 60; Positive - 34 (57%); Negative - 15; Conditional-11.

---

whether they approved of the meeting. While there were more than twice as many positive as negative responses, 43% were either negative or unconvinced about the usefulness of the meeting.

Those who were pleased that it had taken place felt that the ANC had gained recognition and legitimacy as a result, and had been able, against the wishes of Pretoria, to bring its views directly to the attention of the highest levels of the US Government. A trade unionist in Cape Town said:

> For the ANC it was a pure achievement. It gave the Organization a lot of credibility because it reflected the fact that it cannot be ignored as a force. America, the most powerful imperial force in the world, had to talk. There was a massive outcry against the meeting here in Government circles.

A woman community activist, also in Cape Town responded:

> People were absolutely pleased. Thrilled. Why? Reagan and Thatcher vowed they would never talk to "terrorists." But they have been forced to talk, because the ANC is the real representative of our people, even though they are in exile.

According to a young public interest lawyer in Durban:

> It showed that although America still sees the ANC as a terrorist group, at least there has been some change of attitude, and that America has realized that there will be no solution to the problem of this country unless the ANC is consulted, and that it has the large support of people in this country.

A number of people were pleased that "at last" or "for the first time" America at the official level had "heard and seen" the case from the ANC itself. "Now they should know exactly what the ANC is about." Others expressed hope that fighting might stop because talking had begun; the view that some contact is always better than none, "as long as there are no conditions attached;" the opinion that it demonstrated enhanced world attention to South Africa's situation, and to the role of the ANC; and pleasure that it had angered the South African Government.

Others were half-hearted, or expressed mixed feelings, or were suspicious of US motives, or were waiting for something substantial to result from the talks. An employee of UDF explained his view of the meeting:

> I see it as a diplomatic breakthrough for the ANC because it had previously lacked diplomatic access to the US Government. But the US demand that the ANC put an end to its support for violence when violence is one of its major

> strategies sounds almost the same as PW's [Botha's] call to the ANC to renounce violence. Yet there are no other avenues to pursue. I am also dubious [about the meeting] because nothing has happened since. Also the ANC has no control over violence here.

An undergraduate sympathetic to the ANC said he had mixed feelings:

> I did not like the idea of Oliver Tambo meeting there. After so many years they wanted to talk to him. Yet it did prove to the world that they are the legitimate leaders of our people. There can be no settlement in the absence of the ANC. America was forced to have a word with our leaders. I don't know the real American reason for meeting, and I don't know Tambo's exact reason.

A post-graduate student in Johannesburg said:

> Tambo has to be flexible to survive and become widely accepted. So he was right to go. For me, things remain the same. From the American side, I can see that they needed to extend American interests. The American Government feels that the ANC is so important that it could become the government one day and it is therefore worth creating some relationship with it.

A trade union organizer affiliated to the BC-oriented NACTU explained:

> It was done for various reasons. On the part of the ANC it has increased its credibility. However it must be compared with the fact that Buthelezi and Tutu met with President Reagan. In terms of diplomatic signals it is a coup for the ANC. For the US State Department it was under pressure to talk to all parties in order to ward off pressure for disinvestment and sanctions coming from Congress. It was also important for the geo-political role the US wants to play in Mozambique and Zimbabwe that it starts buying friends and influencing people. The State Department also met with a PAC representative before the meeting with Tambo.

A young Inkatha official remarked that he had nothing against the US talking to the ANC as long as it was not recognized as the sole authentic voice of Black South Africans.

Significantly, 25% of the responses were negative. A good deal of the criticism came from BC supporters and sympathizers. A woman in Grahamstown presented this view:

> It demonstrates the arrogance of Whites. People think we should fall over our shoes [with appreciation].... How long could the US postpone it? It is like a situation when someone thinks they are doing you a favor, but it really is an insult.... The ANC can thrive without American recognition. It could be a kind of kiss of death, like [ex-Prime Minister of Rhodesia] Ian Smith wooing Nkomo, a kiss of death.

A young official of Azapo was also critical:

> We believe that America, especially as represented by the Reagan Administration and the Republican Party, will always try to enter negotiations with people they believe represent a factor in a power equation. But we believe that the consultations hinged on the extent to which the ANC is prepared to guarantee certain rights to satisfy the Americans. The Americans are trying to find out what economic system the ANC would implement. And then America can adapt new strategies. They want to influence the ANC in the direction they want.

A man in his thirties, supportive of Azapo, and working for a church-sponsored community organization expressed suspicion:

> I don't remember what the deliberations were about. My blanket opinion is that if America, Britain and Western forces all of a sudden create an interest in a meaningful radical organization then they have something up their sleeves. The best that can come out of that meeting is only to the benefit of the West. I see the Western forces only being interested in a body that they can influence to their way of thinking. I think of their contact with Oliver Tambo as another attempt to lure all our leadership to their way of thinking.

A young woman lawyer explained:

> I don't like the ANC going to talk to America. America is still anti-ANC. It won't support the ANC. So it was a meaningless meeting.

Another lawyer working in Durban added:

> George Shultz met Oliver Tambo, but Ronald Reagan met Buthelezi. Reagan, not Shultz should have met with Tam-

> bo. It is offensive to me. Tambo should not have agreed to meet Shultz. It was not a real gesture [by the Americans].

In addition to BC opinions on this, there were others, mainly from the left of the UDF political spectrum, who were critical. One young man had been in prison at the time and had seen South African newspaper reports of demonstrations in the US accusing the ANC of being communist and opposing the meeting. This was the only report of the meeting that had come through to his cell and it had made him extremely angry. Others based their criticism on more information. A researcher in Natal argued:

> America was worried about the increasing number of people here that are becoming anti-American. It wanted to tell the ANC to stop violence. But it knew the ANC can't abandon violence. It is looking to find some moderates in the ANC like Tambo, a pragmatist and a Christian, to talk to him and change him. The meeting did not amount to anything. Two weeks later it was forgotten. Tambo does not control violence in South Africa. America is now going to cut aid to southern African Governments which support ANC "terrorism." We are angry about this. It shows America is on the side of the South African Government.

A professional, also in Natal, also expressed doubt in America's intentions:

> America has not shown the support it should. They were virtually forced to do this. They would like not to have done this. It has not won any respect from us because it was so begrudgingly done; and the communique showed this. It did create a rift with the South African Government and that is good.

A trade unionist in Cape Town said:

> I did not think about it too much. I don't worry about the ANC. Some of our bosses have also been doing it, going to see the ANC because they will have to work with the ANC. But it hasn't done us any good. So the meeting did not impress us a lot.

Finally on this topic, a graduate student in Johannesburg commented:

> I am happy in the sense that it has revealed the ANC's kinds of future interests - how it understands the situation today and how it sees the future and the role of the US in the South African economy. The interests of the ANC are gradually being revealed by the respect they have shown for an imperialist state. I am critical of the ANC for doing this. It reflects a pure petty-bourgeois tendency. It is not a positive move. I have no hope it will change my future or the future of the majority. It is a betrayal.

d) THE APPOINTMENT OF A BLACK AMBASSADOR

QUESTION: How do you feel about the appointment of a Black American Ambassador to South Africa?

Asked - 63; Negative - 51 (86% of those who expressed an opinion); Positive - 4; Conditional - 4; Don't know - 4.

QUESTION: How do you assess his performance since he has been here?

Asked - 63; Negative - 49 (84% of those who expressed an opinion); Positive - 3; Conditional - 6; Don't know - 5.

The final departure in American policy toward South Africa was the appointment, for the first time, of a Black Ambassador to Pretoria. There had been talk of this earlier in 1986, and I had asked a few members of the first group of interviewees how they would respond to such an appointment. Overwhelmingly they had been negative. It was not surprising therefore to find that when the Reagan Administration went ahead and appointed a Black man, Edward J. Perkins, to the post, the response was hostile. Two questions were put in the second round of interviews: How did you feel about the appointment of a Black Ambassador to South Africa? How do you assess his performance since he has been here? 86% of those who expressed an opinion responded negatively to the first and 84% negatively to the second.

A couple of people, both senior managers in private foundations, were very favorably disposed towards him. One worked in Port Elizabeth:

> I am in favor. He is a very good role model for Black aspirations both here and in America. He has faced discrimination himself and has a Vietnamese wife. He therefore knows discrimination and has experienced it. He is a loveable person. He is not a token. He is the right person at the right place. People have been convinced by his sincerity.

The second was employed in Johannesburg:

> The initial message was one of window-dressing. But since he has come and interacted with the people and taken stances which are not acceptable to Washington. He has gone to the townships and supported small projects. He has become acceptable and removed the initial suspicion.

A trade unionist, working in an affiliate of Cosatu, thought that the idea was a good one, but was critical of the Ambassador's performance.

> It was a wise move by the US Government because you can't deny the fact that one of the ways people gauge America is the way they treat Black Americans. Also the appointment of a Black Ambassador sends a message to Black South Africans that you could be this and achieve this if things in South Africa change. So it has a message for some sections of the Black community - those sections vying for those positions. But he hasn't done anything since he is here.

There were a few answers which, while critical, nevertheless acknowledged that there may have been a positive element somewhere, or that the Ambassador might have been learning. For example, a physician noted that the Ambassador had made overtures to the UDF, and that some of his statements "sounded reasonable. He has a less negative effect on us than Nichols." Herman Nichols was Perkins' predecessor. From my 1986 interviews I had gathered that there was extremely strong antagonism felt towards Nichols, and many prominent Blacks refused to meet personally with him. I had not specifically asked about him, but I think it would be fair to summarize the comments they volunteered about Nichols as follows: He was a Reagan appointee (already a bad start), carrying out Reagan's policies (which were bad), badly. As far this group was concerned, he was the wrong person at the wrong moment. In this situation it was likely that any new Ambassador, irrespective of color, would have been seen as an improvement. A doctoral student asserted that the appointment was aimed at deceiving Black Americans, which irritated him. He went on to note with approval a recent speech by the Ambassador that American companies should be disinvesting. "Maybe he is improving and increasing his understanding". A Nactu-affiliated trade union official commented:

> To us personally it was a moment of anger that he actually wanted to accept the position. We talked to American Black leaders to try to dissuade him. Nothing significant has changed since he arrived.... He is very quiet. He might just be more astute - maybe he is taking his time before he launches in; and it is strategically important for him to keep quiet at first. He has been going out on visits to Black communities.

For the rest, both the appointment and the performance were negatively assessed. It was seen as a "propaganda ploy" which "helps him further his own career interests," as "insulting," "irritating," "opportunistic," "meaningless," etc. "People no longer see things in Black-White terms only. So if they think we are excited they are wrong," a university lecturer explained. "Black or White he remains an extension of imperialism," was another response. "Color is irrelevant," said a Johannesburg businessman. "He is American and so we don't expect much." A manager in Port Elizabeth analyzed the situation in this way:

> If the Democrats sent him with the support of Black people it would be a good thing. But this Ambassador came against the will of Blacks in the US. For him to be here on behalf of the present US Government is of no benefit to Black South Africans. It might be of benefit to Buthelezi but not others. Only politically non-involved people met with him. When a Democratic Ambassador was here he was very helpful and we trusted him. People are very disappointed in him. It is difficult to say if he is doing a good job, because I don't know what he is doing.

A teacher in Grahamstown said:

> It is not meaningful. Color does not count. Black or White he carries the same orders. It is a humiliating practice. It is a clear sign that Americans think we are stupid. It shows how Ronald Reagan sees South Africa. He sees it all divided into ethnic groups - he talks just like the South African Government - for example about "the Zulu nation." [Perkins] hasn't done anything. All organizations in the Eastern Cape rejected his presence. He came at the wrong time when people were in detention. So, who does he speak to?

An employee of an educational organization in Natal also made the case that it was a meaningless gesture. He still represented "Constructive Engagement," the same regional policy and unchanged support for Unita. "I've been in detention most of the time and he didn't do anything about detentions." A woman lawyer saw it as a public relations exercise similar to South Africa appointing an Indian as Ambassador to the European Economic Community. "It is a typically South African thing. Birds of a feather." This comparison with Pretoria's appointment of a non-White Ambassador was repeated by a few people. An Azapo official said that Perkins had allowed himself to be used by the Reagan Administration (and, he added, his organization had conveyed this view directly to the Ambassador), and had in the process "become a dupe, a goon." An educationist in Grahamstown described the appointment as "like giving sweets to children. It is insulting. We keep clear of him. We pity him as a Black brother." Even though opponents of Inkatha attacked the Ambassador for giving too much attention to Buthelezi, Inkatha interviewees were as negative about him as anyone else.

Interestingly, amidst all this criticism of his performance, a number of his detractors acknowledged one positive action he had taken: while they mentioned different actions, nobody mentioned more than one. "He attended a mass meeting organized by the UDF, and afterwards gave a statement at a press conference condemning the South African Government." "He did once respond by making a statement on detentions." "He has travelled and talked and listened." "He did speak out against the detention of kids and a few people appreciated that." "In a recent speech in America he spoke out in favor of companies disinvesting, and went further than the White House wanted him to go." "He attended the Delmas trial to show concern - other embassies also attended - and this may have helped ensure justice in the court." If one adds these actions together he has clearly done a bit more than he is given credit for. This does not however detract from the overall negative evaluation of both the decision to post him to Pretoria and of his performance up until that stage.

Such was the level of antagonism felt towards the Reagan Presidency, and the policies it continued to pursue that this perception of a Reagan appointee should not be surprising.

The combined impact of the four policy changes and their implications for the Study will be analyzed in the final chapter.

NOTES

* Because of the nature of the questions and answers on these two issues of sanctions and disinvestment the numbers referred to in sections a) and b) of this chapter are not considered significant. Quantities are used here because they convey more clearly than general terms such as "many" or "few" the views of the members of the group.

1. Reagan Urged to Stiffen S. African Sanctions, *Washington Post* (10/2/87).

2. William Minter, "South Africa: Straight Talk on Sanctions," *Foreign Policy*, 65 (1896-87): 48 and 49.

3. Some Gaps and Some Silences in Cosatu's Disinvestment Call, *Weekly Mail* (7/24/87): 17.

4. See note 3.

5. "Cosatu's 2nd National Congress Press Release," Johannesburg (Saturday 18 July 1987).

> has not been a lot of thought from either side. First, we had a good relationship between the two Governments; now we have a complete turnabout.

A priest commented:

> Yes, there is a change in the attitude of the American Government to take the South African situation more seriously. Yet very emphatically we say that they could be doing more. It could be a first step, but we are anxious about time. They have to put pressure. The Group Areas Act must be lifted now. In 5 years it will be too late.

An Inkatha officer added:

> It is a big change. America wants to see South Africa change. In their minds they thought they were doing this for the good of South Africa, yet we think it is for the bad, because disinvestment can't be good for the Blacks of South Africa. So now I am less positive. It is a big difference in my mind.

Second, these are some examples of people who were of the opinion that there had been a small change in US policy. To begin with, these are the words of a manager in Port Elizabeth:

> Reagan wants to put his finger in each and every pie. The Black Ambassador did not change people's opinions, but the majority thought that the meeting with Tambo was a step in the right direction. I am not an ANC supporter. On disinvestment and on sanctions, Reagan wants to veto anything detrimental to his personal views. He is in cahoots with the South African Government, and therefore he vetoes. It does not add up to a significant change in US policy, although somehow it is slightly altered.

A works supervisor in a private organization responded to the question in this way:

> It does amount to a change. In domestic politics in America some groups are sincere and put pressure. [Ambassador] Perkins is not an improvement because he arrived in response to a crisis. The pace is very slow. There should be an ANC office in America. It is a beginning. Yet we are angry because America is fighting with Russia, and using South Africa for this.

A teacher in Grahamstown expressed partial approval:

> I liked the meeting with Tambo the most. It had an impact. There is a change but it is a very slow cautious change. The US doesn't do here what it does against other countries. Elsewhere it has had an impact, for example in Poland, but not here. I personally feel just the same about their policy. The meeting was important but it does not go anywhere. Sanctions seems like a government thing, but it doesn't affect the corporations. For example, flights to America - people get around it.

A technical assistant, recently released from detention, had this to say:

> There is a little bit of change. The meeting with Tambo was meaningful. America is making a hell of a lot of money here; so they need to talk to the ANC. But there were no results. So it doesn't make me any less critical because of what actually transpired at the meeting, and nothing came of it. So I've become more critical because America is linked to South Africa and they don't do anything to force South Africa to end apartheid.

A university research associate also commented:

> There seems to be a dent in the old image. It is the beginning of a process of change. I'll wait and see if I change my mind. They still have not supported the ANC. They still support Unita. It is full of contradictions.... They all seem to be saying different things.

A physician said:

> It signifies some change, and shows the effects of public pressure and a Democratic victory in Congress on the right wing role that Reagan has played. I think that they had to accept the ANC as one of the authoritative voices of South African Black people. The US is going to try to use its muscle to bring the ANC to the negotiating table. I don't see them supporting the genuine emergence of a democratic movement in this country. There is no change in my perception of US policy, but I do make a distinction between Reagan and other domestic forces in the US. Anything short of the extreme right-wing is better. But I am very doubtful about how far Congress will go because of their obsession with communists in the ANC.

A paralegal adviser agreed that there was limited change:

> Yes, there is a realization by the Americans that the Nationalists are the wrong horse to back. Till now they put their money on the White population. They did not believe the liberation movement was strong enough to take over. They want to be in a position to put someone in power who is pro-Western. So they have moved slightly, in order to back both horses. I am not less critical at all.

A trade unionist made a similar point, arguing that the US wanted to be more acceptable to the ANC in order to keep capitalism and exploitation going in a post-apartheid system. Similarly, a graduate student claimed that the advances of the resistance movement had forced capitalism to see that apartheid was no longer good for business. Another student felt that because the changes had been forced on the American leadership it would do its best to negate the gains. All of these four people, while acknowledging limited change, asserted that they had either retained their earlier view or become more rather than less critical of the US in consequence.

Thirdly, there follows a selection of comments by those interviewed who felt that there had been no meaningful change in US policy at all. A manager argued that the actions taken were purely symbolic and resulted from shareholder pressure on companies. "There was no intention to push Pretoria to dismantle apartheid." A businessman referred to it as "politicking" and "peripheral" to the main issues. "We are just pawns on a chessboard.... We are wasting time." At more length a Johannesburg journalist explained why he saw no change:

> America is saying there has been a shift from Constructive Engagement, but America is pumping millions of dollars into Unita. Whatever it is giving with the right hand it is taking away with the left hand. My attitude has not changed at all. Quite honestly it has been influenced by what America does elsewhere even more than what it does here. Here we have a Government that is doing what

> America would be doing anyway. So they don't need to be visible here. But they are elsewhere, in destabilizing all over, and they are in Nicaragua. We have learnt to distrust America so that even this slight shift we view with a lot of suspicion. America is very good at studying and watching which way the wind is blowing, and then they support whoever they think will be the winner. At the time that they thought that the South African Government was firmly in control, they used Constructive Engagement. The situation has been changing. Pressure is mounting on the Government everyday. You get the feeling that the Government will have to give into some of the demands, and so America wants to give the impression that it is siding with the Blacks. The shift is very cautious.... A lot of American dollars are being pumped into this country to win over young Blacks ... who are being sent to America in large numbers; also to Britain. On the surface one would say that it looks good - there is nothing wrong with assistance for education - but we can't close our eyes to what we see as very dishonest motives for granting that kind of assistance. We are watching them with suspicion.

A student, a Nactu-affiliated union organizer and an engineer all made similar points about imperialism adapting so as to "look for safeguards" for its interests, and "hijack the struggle" in order to continue getting their capital out and to create a permanent dependence on imperialism. Because of the nature of imperialism these adaptations could not by definition amount to meaningful change for Black South Africans. A Cosatu-affiliated unionist made the case that this "diplomacy" had no meaning for the man in the street. The Government had become more repressive. There had been three states of emergency, continuation of apartheid in the Group Areas Act, punitive measures against squatter communities, a clamp down on the news, mass detentions, torture and a deteriorating situation for those living in the homelands. Another view was that the action of meeting Tambo was to satisfy a particular lobby in the US, not to influence change in South Africa. The significance of the measures was said by a number of people to have been reduced by the routine calls for the ANC to renounce violence, despite the fact that the Administration knew that the ANC did not choose violence as a strategy but had been left with no choice but to engage in armed struggle, and continued to ignore the continual use of violence by the South African Government. "But still they say it must renounce violence. Even when people are dying left and right, and the townships are like army camps, they don't say anything about that except to send a Black Ambassador."

The threat to cut off aid to the southern African Front Line States that supported organizations engaging in violence and necklacing - a 1987 US Congressional amendment seen as specifically intended to weaken the ANC - angered these people yet further. A university lecturer explained why his attitude had not altered:

> Its view of the ANC is the same. Now it is even more scathing about the ANC. The US is aware that the ANC is widely supported and is an alternative potential government. Their fear is of the ANC's connections with the Communist Party and the socialist line. Now they have threatened the Front Line States that they must not support terrorism ... I have the same view exactly of the US as I had last year. We shall only see real effective sanctions if we get a popular government in South Africa, particularly if it is socialist; but not now because the US is benefitting a hell of a lot from apartheid.

Reagan's resistance to the sanctions legislation was also said to make it less meaningful and to mean that it was less likely to be implemented effectively. There were pleas for him to denounce apartheid unequivocally, and to challenge more aggressively the Government on its use of violence, and for Secretary Shultz to talk directly to Pretoria about changing its laws.

b) COMPARING THE TWO ROUNDS OF INTERVIEWS

Taking into account the responses to these two questions and the detailed comparisons contained in the three tables, with their accompanying sets of comments (See Tables 9, 10, and 11 in the Apendix), one may make the following summary: 89% of the second group felt that their own sense of hostility toward the US had not been reduced, 5% said they were less critical, 2% wanted to wait and see, and 6% gave conditional answers. This seems fairly accurately to reflect the results of the three tables, in which three different methods of comparing the findings of the two years were used. The key observation - given the alterations in US policy - is how little change there had been. The minor observation is that for a very small minority there had been a slight reduction in hostility toward the US.

c) ANALYZING THE TWO ROUNDS: PERCEPTIONS UNCHANGED

In 1986, some of the major criticisms of the US related to the Administration's failure to apply sanctions, consult the ANC and push for disinvestment of US corporations. These failings formed an essential part of the basis of antagonism felt towards the American Government. It would seem, on the surface at least, that in the course of the intervening year that the US had gone some way toward satisfying those demands. Very clearly, however, these steps had made precious little impact on Black attitudes to America. This Conclusion will first attempt to suggest explanations for the lack of impact and the continuing hostility.

President Reagan's opposition to the Sanctions Law and to disinvestment detracted from its impact on Black South Africans. The fact that Congress took the unusual step of overriding the President's veto, was not seen as a victory. This may result from a notion of South African political processes where the State President is all-powerful and Parliament is comparatively weak; if a decision were ever to be taken without his support it would be very unlikely to make any headway. Also it did mean that the most important leader in the US both substantively and symbolically was opposed to these actions and they therefore carried less weight. Black South Africans were obviously suspicious of the sincerity with which the law would be implemented under these circumstances. It would seem that in this regard they had good reasons for doubt since many of the provisions have not been put into practice, or have been interpreted in such a way as to restrict their impact.

The fact that corporations have disinvested under pressure both political and economic, rather than doing so in order to strengthen the cause of liberation, has reduced their meaning for Black South Africans. There was a widely held view that companies are leaving because profits were down, or they were under threat of losing business abroad. Again while this could be interpreted as a victory for the pressures building up in South Africa and abroad, this did not seem to be the way it was being interpreted amongst many educated Blacks in South Africa.

The manner in which disinvestment has been taking place has strengthened these doubts. Management sellouts to local White managers, or to Anglo-American or to foreign companies, at discounted prices and with all production systems and licensing arrangements continuing, have meant that disinvestment has turned out to be a very different process from that anticipated. Corporations were not leaving; no crisis was resulting; pressure on the Government was not that significant; some White businessmen were in fact benefitting; and some Black workers, probably not many in number yet, were suffering. Blacks called for a particular type of action against apartheid. They felt they had been tricked. Capital had circumvented their intentions while cynically claiming credit for having responded to their call. Suspicion of the role of capitalism, so strongly expressed in the first round of interviews, was not reduced by these actions.

There were probably exaggerated expectations of the consequences of sanctions and disinvestment. Even operating effectively, which they were not, they would take time to bite into the economy. Exaggerated too would be the sense of America's control over its Western allies such as Britain, Japan and West Germany. Even if the US pushed its allies to cooperate, which the Law required the President to do, but which it failed to do, it does not have that much influence. This is not to say it could not have done much more than it did. Nevertheless, once it became clear that results were going to take a long time, disappointment set in quickly.

The Administration's continuing call on the ANC to renounce violence continued to cause hostility. It was widely seen in the following terms: as selective, since the US itself uses violence when it deems this necessary and supports violence when it thinks it is advantageous to its interests; the US should by now be aware that Black South Africans have a very long history of peaceful resistance which made no headway; as unrealistic given the Government's handling of Black opposition; and ultimately as serving as an excuse for refusing to support the movement. The Congressional amendment in mid-1987 calling on Front Line States to also renounce violence and threatening them with discontinuation of aid exacerbated this sense of anger. As they interpreted this, the ultimate objective must have been to weaken the effectiveness of South Africa's and Namibia's liberation movements.

The overt support given to Unita continued to cause a great deal of anger among Black South Africans. This was based on a decision of Congress, not only of the President, and was seen as putting the US firmly into a military alliance with the South African Government. For some, it was therefore difficult to see how the US could sincerely oppose the Government when it has chosen to fight on the same side. Whatever other steps the US might take in the region, say in support of SADCC, would remain suspect as long the support for Unita continued. Clearly, the peace accord on Namibia and Angola, negotiated by the US, may make a positive impression on Black South Africans.

Educated Black South Africans have also come increasingly to identify with other third world peoples and countries. In particular the Reagan Administration's support of the Contras in Nicaragua caused considerable concern. The bombing of Libya, too, caused resentment. The approach to the Palestinian question was being increasingly criticized. Some people made the point as well that if South Africa were ever to be a popular democracy or a socialist society it would face up to the same US response as Nicaragua.

Capitalism, with which America is so closely identified, was under increasing suspicion in South Africa. As this Study has made clear, Blacks were coming to identify capitalism with apartheid. In tandem these systems have exploited them for a long time. There were those who made the point that true private enterprise did not operate in the country. Nevertheless, most people interviewed did appear to identify the system as capitalist and to feel that it had brought very few benefits to Black South Africans. Those among the interviewees who identified America as imperialist therefore went on to make the case that America would not willingly undermine a capitalist system from which it was profiting.

Anger toward the US has been growing for some time now, possibly for a decade, and more particularly since the Reagan Administration came to office. The reasons for this change in attitude emerge from the interviews. Suspicion was therefore high. Ulterior motives for any apparently positive move were therefore always sought. Scholarships and aid for community projects were seen by some as aimed at coopting Black South Africans to the US cause. At least as long as President Reagan was in office no improvement was anticipated.

American politicians were also seen as overly concerned with the communist threat in South Africa - and elsewhere. It was therefore anticipated that the US would continue in the main to stand on the side of those whom its leaders judged most likely to reliably support capitalism and oppose communism in the future. In general those interviewed did not see the South African Communist Party as having much impact in the future. What they did feel was that the US trusted the White Government and White business community to ensure the continuation of capitalism and that the US would therefore continue to support the fundamentals of the status quo. They also saw the fuss about communist influence as a further stratagem for refusing to back the ANC.

Finally - in explaining the persistence of these negative perceptions of the US - the history of events over the previous 24 months inside South Africa would have affected the response. The South African Government had effectively and cruelly delayed the progress of the Black struggle. There has been a great deal of suffering. This may be only a temporary setback. But in the meantime Blacks looked around and saw increased oppression and a deteriorating political situation, and they must have come to the conclusion that whatever foreign powers were doing, it was having no positive impact.

d) THE NATURE OF ANTI-AMERICANISM

In attempting to understand more of the nature of anti-Americanism among Black South Africans it may be useful to refer to the comparative framework suggested by Alvin Rubinstein and Donald Smith.[1] They suggest four possible areas of disagreement which might give rise to third world anti-Americanism. First, there is US global policy which is perceived as being so obsessed with the threat of communism that it is ready to sacrifice third world interests to counteract what it sees as communist advances. Second, there is US policy toward the third world itself: the US is seen as preeminently a status quo power siding with, and intervening on behalf of (to protect or reinstate), vested interests. Third, there is American economic activity in the third world which is characterized as US-based multinationals continuing to exploit their economies. Fourth, there are a range of negative perceptions of US society which they either disapprove of or feel threatened by.

Clearly in our Study the prime cause of hostility was not generalized US policies but US policy toward South Africa itself. This was seen as supportive of the South African Government and as a hindrance to Black liberation. It is obvious however from the responses described in this Study that the other potential areas of disagreement were becoming increasingly relevant. Many of those interviewed made the point about US obsession with communism being at the basis of US - and particularly Reagan's - policies toward South Africa. Its disaffection with the ANC and its support for Unita in Angola were given as examples. There was also growing awareness of, and antagonism toward, US interventions in the third world. There was almost universal criticism of the US role in Nicaragua and in Angola, and many in the group criticized US involvement in Vietnam and Grenada and the bombing of Libya. Part of the radicalization process at work amongst Black South Africans includes a growing identification with third world countries and movements seen as being under pressure from the US. Also part of the radicalization process was an enhanced understanding of and antipathy toward capitalism as it operates in South Africa. While this was based primarily on a negative assessment of corporate behavior in South Africa itself, there was a broadening sense - based as much on projected analogy as on information - of a shared third world experience of exploitation by US capitalism. Of less significance than the other areas of disagreement with the US was that based on perceptions of US society. There were those in the group who were critical and they included some Black Consciousness supporters concerned about protecting the authenticity and communal nature of African life, and others who pointed to the miserable conditions of the American under-class, mainly Black, which they saw as an inevitable consequence of an exploitative economic system. But the majority of the group were generally fairly positive about the nature of the American system. This did not mean that they wanted to copy it in South Africa, but it was not a major source of anti-Americanism.

Rubinstein and Smith also present a four-part typology of anti-Americanism. Issue-oriented anti-Americanism is founded on opposition to specific policies and practices of the US in the third world. Ideological anti-Americanism is a sustained antagonism to the government and society of the US forming part of a broader belief system. Instrumental anti-Americanism describes the instigation or manipulation of hostility toward the US by governments with ulterior motives, such as deflecting attention away from domestic problems. Revolutionary anti-Americanism is found in a situation in which a revolutionary movement is striving to overthrow a US-supported government.

It would be difficult to assess the extent of instrumental anti-Americanism among Black South African leadership. Clearly, in a situation in which there has been such limited progress made, there must be a temptation to blame outside forces. Instrumental anti-Americanism may be have been one component of the overall phenomenon, but it was not a major one. Black South Africans were very forthright about acknowledging the military and economic might of the Government and their own relative weakness. They also consistently stressed that the struggle was essentially their own responsibility and all that they hoped for was assistance and support from the outside world. The other three forms that hostility takes, namely, issue-oriented, ideological and revolutionary, may be seen as distinct categories or as interrelated stages on a continuum. As regards categories it would be impossible to generalize: as can be discerned from the responses the anti-Americanism of some was issue-oriented, while for others it was ideological. If one thinks in terms of interrelated stages it was clear that the issue oriented and the ideological forms of anti-Americanism were feeding into and enhancing one another. For example, the way in which the Reagan Administration handled sanctions, President Reagan's speeches on South Africa, and the withdrawal of aid from Zimbabwe, etc., all came to form a pattern in the mind of Black South African observers, a pattern which increasingly paralleled the expectations generated by the ideological anti-Americanism. It was of course the growing ideological influence which in turn facilitated their discernment of such patterns. They were interdependent and self-reinforcing, and steadily becoming part of a revolutionary anti-Americanism: increasingly politicized Black South Africans were seeing the US Government as a partner of the South African Government, a partnership which in their minds demonstrated the essential linkage between capitalism and apartheid. This process seemed destined to strengthen during the rest of the Reagan era. Clearly they had given up hope of change emanating from his Administration.

e) CONCLUSION: OF REAGANISM AND RADICALISM

The comparative analysis of the two rounds of interviews and the discussion of Rubinstein and Smith's notions of anti-Americanism take us some way toward answering the main questions raised by the simple model of revolution, radicalism and anti-Americanism suggested in the first chapter of this book.

There can be no doubt whatever that over the previous ten or fifteen years there had been a dramatic increase in anti-American sentiment among educated urban Black South Africans. This was not only among "radicals." And, as the preceding discussion in section c) of this chapter demonstrates, this antagonism was not a passing phase. It was felt as strongly by professional people, senior managers, and businessmen as by trade unionists and community organizers, and as much by middle-aged as by younger people. Older people talked of their hopes of a decade (and more) ago that America would inevitably come to their assistance. They felt very disappointed. Young people spoke of cultural imperialism contained in their high school materials which had influenced them to view the US in a very favorable light; now they said they had seen through it. With the exception of the supporters of Inkatha, the predominant perception of the people interviewed was that the US was a hindrance and not a help to their struggle.

The depth of antagonism toward, and disappointment with, President Reagan felt by middle class Blacks who were in favor of capitalism was noteworthy. This raises the question of the causal links included in the model. If capitalist middle class Blacks were antagonistic this might suggest no more than a broad sense of despair at the policies of the Reagan Administration which might not be directly linked to growing radicalism of any particular nature. One must accept that this has validity. The President himself and his long-established record and image, and what were seen as his inopportune declarations (about South Africa and Angola), his Assistant Secretary of State for Africa, Chester Crocker, their policy of Constructive Engagement, their opposition to sanctions and disinvestment, hostility to the ANC, vetoes at the UN and failure for so long to press Pretoria on Namibian independence undoubtedly provided a major cause for the negative attitudes described.

There were other reasons too which do not in the first instance point to more basic changes in analysis. For one, the control of the media by the South African Government and by large business interests affects the way Blacks look at the world: in most instances it has the opposite effect from that intended. Reading, listening and viewing Black South Africans so distrusted the media that their first instinct was not merely to "read between the lines, but to think exactly the opposite." Their initial views on Qaddafi, Afghanistan and Poland were all influenced by this. In addition, the sort of logic which follows the lines: "the enemy of my enemy is my friend and the friend of my enemy is my enemy" is also of importance in understanding reactions. This emerged in some of the interviewees' attitudes to the Palestinian issue, the US bombing of Libya and Unita's war in Angola, and of course, to the US itself. Qaddafi gave support to Black South Africans, and the US bombed Qaddafi. Unita and the South African Defence Force were allies, and the US sent Unita military assistance. Israel cooperated closely with South Africa and the US was Israel's closest and most important ally. And so on. This is not to suggest that analysis stopped at this point - and the change in the assessment of the Solidarity experience is evidence of that - but it was nevertheless influential in the early orientation of perceptions of countries and conflicts. When reaction to, transforms into analysis of, say the role of the press and of international alliances, as was occurring among these Black South Africans, a process of radicalization needs to be acknowledged.

There is ample evidence in these interviews that changes that go much deeper than mere disapproval of an American President's policies were occurring. As we saw in Chapters 5 and 6 there were different notions of what radicalism meant; nevertheless 64 out of the 74 people asked (86%) agreed and only one disagreed that radicalism was growing among Black South Africans. Further, 51 out of the 58 asked (88%) said that an acceptance of violence as necessary for change had also increased. Only 4 disagreed. There was also a very strong anti-capitalist trend. This was most clearly discernible among trade unionists and younger activists and organizers, and it was strongest among Black Consciousness sympathizers and the left of the UDF. But it went beyond these categories to include some professional and middle-aged people. And even those who believed in private enterprise acknowledged that a substantial change in the distribution of resources would be required in a post-apartheid South Africa. It was obvious to all that capitalism as it has operated in South Africa has long exploited and damaged Black people. Differences did exist however over whether capitalism, freed of apartheid, might serve Black peoples' interests. The majority of the group interviewed seemed to think that those Black South Africans who were aware of the issues involved no longer thought that this was likely.

There was also broad consensus that a positive interest in socialist alternatives was growing. The same groups that were felt to be most anti-capitalist were also thought to be the most interested in socialism. While this was acknowledged to amount to a definite change in view from say 10 or 15 years before, it was not clear yet how strongly these views were held, nor what people actually had in their minds when they spoke of socialism. What was clear was that it was growing and that the organizations and types of people who were most likely to be supportive - namely the workers and their unions, and the youth and their organizations - were also those who were most likely to provide the main thrust of Black opposition to apartheid in the future.

My own impression of the growth in anti-capitalist sentiment and interest in socialism was that this did not have much to do with ANC influence; and even less with the make-up of the ANC executive. It seemed to be based on internal organizations, experiences and responses, and the analyses that were evolving in reaction to, and as explanations for, those experiences. Unlike the wars of liberation referred to in the opening chapter, namely in Mozambique, Angola and Zimbabwe, this struggle has not so far followed the model of a prolonged rural conflict in which liberated zones are established and in which the main liberation movement structures an ideological hegemony. Here it seems the most dynamic source of ideological analysis and experimentation is in the urban areas among organizers and leaders supportive of, but not necessarily dependent upon, the ANC. So while the geographic and organizational base of this liberation struggle diverges somewhat from that of neighboring countries' experiences, the pattern of ideological evolution clearly has similarities.

Radicalism was on the increase, at the same time as Black Consciousness appeared to be on the decline. The ANC's influence in favor of non-racial analyses, strategies and objectives appeared to be significant. Also of relevance was a growing acceptance among intellectuals and leaders of the analytical potential of class analysis to the comprehension and future solution of their predicament. The BC's own analysis is now far more clearly focused on class than on race. This tendency is significant to an appreciation of what is happening. There may be an interpretation of the anti-capitalist trend as no more than a knee-jerk and mainly rhetorical reaction to Pretoria's declared dedication to uphold capitalism. It must be reemphasized however that Pretoria's discriminatory segregation practices have used race as the basis of division: *Black* people have over the years been kept out of *White* jobs, schools, suburbs, trains, hospitals, rest rooms, etc., as Blacks or non-Whites, not as workers. From rest room signs to passbooks reference has been to race, not to class. Therefore a movement that reaches beyond race in its efforts to understand and find a way forward has to be seen as operating at an analytical level that goes far beyond the knee-jerk reaction suggested. Also going beyond the purely reactive was the commitment to non-alignment and the retention of autonomy from the USSR, despite a definite appreciation of Soviet assistance.

There was, then, growing radicalism (which appeared to be increasingly divorced from Black Consciousness and increasingly identified with international concerns), anti-capitalism, and signs of pro-socialism. There was, too, anti-Americanism. Is there a causal connection? Is the model suggested in the Introduction appropriate? The answer is not simple, nor is it uni-directional, nor is it in any way final; but it is "yes." It is not simple, because the growing anti-capitalism and, more particularly, the more positive interest in socialism, were both still at an early, rather ill-formed stage of development; and while they were undoubtedly already influencing perceptions of the US, it would be premature to conclude that the analyses on which they were based provide the main force for anti-Americanism. The policies of the American Government played at least as great a part in achieving this negative assessment. It is in this sense that the relationship should not be seen as uni-directional. Constructive Engagement, as propounded and practiced by the Reagan Administration, has done much to radicalize Blacks and facilitate their seeing a connection between Western - particularly US - capitalist interests and the South African Government. Many a radical South African would have to acknowledge an educative debt to President Reagan for having facilitated the conscientization of Black South Africans about these linkages. And lastly, while advancing, this process was not final. "This is not past the point of no return," one woman said to me. "If socialism hasn't arrived when our freedom arrives," said another, "we won't have to be carried screaming and kicking through the door." Whether the trends discerned in this Study continue will depend on many factors; US policy toward South Africa and the region will be one.

NOTES

1. Alvin Z. Rubinstein and Donald E. Smith (eds), *Anti-Americanism in the Third World. Implications for U.S. Foreign Policy* (New York: Praeger, 1985), points selected from Chapter 1.

APPENDICES

TABLE 2 SCHLEMMER: WORKERS' SUPPORT FOR POLITICAL ORGANIZATIONS

	Witwatersrand/ Port Elizabeth		Durban	
ANC/Nelson Mandela	27% -	37.0%*	11% -	11.5%*
UDF	11	15.1	23	24.5
Azaso**	1	1.4	1	1.1
Azapo	5	6.8	1	1.1
Inkatha/Buthelezi	14	19.2	54	56.3
Sofasonke	15	20.5	6	6.3
Other	5		4	
None	22		-	

* as a percentage omitting Other and None
** Azanian Students' Organization

ADAPTING SCHLEMMER

ANC/UDF includes: ANC/Mandela + UDF + Azaso

Sofasonke is a Soweto-centered group. Even if given a more generic meaning of people willing to work within Government urban structures, 15% as an average for Witwatersrand/Port Elizabeth appears very high. To balance this to some extent it will be given a zero in "Cape Town."

Inkatha is very weak in Port Elizabeth, which means it must have come close to 25% in the Witwatersrand, which also appears high. To balance this to some extent it will be given a zero in "Cape Town," where its support is small.

In order to make this comparable with the other two surveys Cape Town will be added notionally by using the Witwatersrand/Port Elizabeth figures and giving 4/5 of the Sofasonke and Inkatha support to ANC/UDF and 1/5 to BC/NF/Azapo; and it will be assumed that Port Elizabeth and Witwatersrand returned identical results.

=

	W-srand	Port El	Durban	"Cape Town"	Overall
ANC/UDF	53.5	53.5	37.1	85.3	57.4
BC/NF/Azapo	6.8	6.8	1.1	14.7	7.4
Inkatha	19.0	19.0	56.3	-	23.6
Sofasonke	20.5	20.5	6.3	-	11.8

TABLE 3 MEER: POLITICAL CHOICES IN FOUR METROPOLITAN AREAS

UDF	23.5%	29.0%*
ANC	20.0	25.0
Azapo	10.1	12.5
Socialist	6.7	8.3
Prog Fed Party	6.4	7.9
Inkatha	3.5	4.3
Christian	3.3	4.0
Nationalist	2.7	3.3
PAC	2.6	3.2
Communist	2.0	2.5
Other/None	19.2	

* as a percentage omitting Other and None

ADAPTING MEER

ANC/UDF includes UDF + ANC + 3/4 Socialist + 2/3 Prog Fed Party + 2/3 Christian + 3/4 Communist

BC/NF/Azapo includes Azapo + 1/4 Socialist + PAC + 1/4 Communist

Inkatha includes Inkatha + 1/3 Prog Fed Party + 1/3 Christian

=

ANC/UDF	29 + 25 + 6.3 + 5.3 + 2.7 + 1.5	=	69.8%
BC/NF/Azapo	12.5 + 2.1 + 3.2 + 0.5	=	18.3
Inkatha	4.3 + 2.6 + 1.3	=	8.2
Government	3.3	=	3.3

TABLE 4 ORKIN: URBAN BLACK SUPPORT FOR POLITICAL TENDENCIES

Tendency	Subtotal %	Item %	*
Nelson Mandela & ANC	31%		40.2%
Nelson Mandela		23	29.9
ANC		8	10.4
UDF & radical groups	14		18.2
UDF		8	10.4
Azapo/Azasm		1	1.3
Dr Allan Boesak		1	1.3
Cosas/Azaso		1	1.3
PAC		1	1.3
SACC		1	1.3
Trade unions		1	1.3
Bishop Desmond Tutu	16	16	20.1
Chief Buthelezi & Inkatha	8		10.4
Chief Buthelezi		6	7.8
Inkatha		2	2.6
Government & pro-investment groupings	8		10.4
PW Botha/Government		5	6.5
Community Councillors		2	2.6
White opposition		1	1.3
Sundry	24		
Don't know		8	
Other		3	
None/No leader		13	

* as a percentage omitting Sundry

ADAPTING ORKIN

UDF excludes Azapo/Azasm and PAC
ANC/UDF includes Mandela & ANC + UDF & radical groups + Tutu - Azapo/Azasm - PAC

BC/NF/Azapo includes Azapo/Azasm + PAC

Inkatha includes Buthelezi & Inkatha

TABLE 4 continued

=

ANC/UDF	40.2 + 18.2 + 20.1 - 1.3 - 1.3	= 75.9%
BC/NF/Azapo	1.3 + 1.3	= 2.6
Inkatha	10.4	= 10.4
Government & pro-investment	10.4	= 10.4

TABLE 5: POLITICAL SUPPORT OF THE GROUP INTERVIEWED

Tendency	1986	1987	Total	%
ANC/UDF/Charterists	33	31	64	69.8
BC/NF/Azapo	6	7	13	14.0
Inkatha	4	5	9	9.7
"Distanced" from ANC	2	2	4	4.3
Mixed ANC/UDF & BC/NF	0	3	3	3.2

TABLE 6: AGE DISTRIBUTION OF THE GROUP

Age category	1986	1987	Total	%
Over 50	8	1	9	9.7
40 - 49	9	11	20	21.5
30 - 39	17	18	35	37.6
Under 30	13	16	29	31.2

TABLE 7: EDUCATION LEVELS OF THE GROUP

Level	1986	1987	Total	%
University graduates	24	23	47*	50.5
Undergraduates	3	2	5	5.4
Completed most/all high school	18	23	41	44.1

TABLE 8: OCCUPATIONS OF THE GROUP

Occupation	1986	1987	Total	%
Foundation managers	6	5	11	11.8
Middle-level managers	2	2	4	4.3
Senior corporation managers	4	0	4	4.3
Businessmen	2	1	3	3.2
Academics	4	3	7	7.5
University students	6	5	11	11.8
Journalists	1	1	2	2.2
Lawyers	1	6	7	7.5
Medical doctors	1	1	2	2.2
Priests	2	1	3	3.2
Trade unionists	7	10	17	18.3

Full-time political organizers	2	4	6	6.5
Community/Voluntary organizers	5	5	10	10.8
Technical assistants/ secretaries	2	1	3	3.2
Others (engineer,teacher, unemployed)	0	3	3	3.2

TABLE 9 COMPARING FIRST AND SECOND ROUND ANSWERS

%age

QUESTION	'86	'87	'86	'87	'86	'87	'86	'87
	asked/who answered		yes/ positive		no/ negative		condi- tional	
1 Importance of US	100	100	95	77	0	15	5	8
2 Personal assess- ment critical	100	100	96	81	4	15	0	4
3 Personal assess- ment increasing- ly critical	100	100	77	60	21	38	3	2
4 Distinguish Demo- crats and Repub- licans	88	76	39	41	34	55	26	3
5 SA Blacks anti- American	98	96	86	80	2	11	11	9
6 SA Blacks in- creasingly anti- American	97	98	84	77	5	13	11	11
7 Radicalism increasing	97	100	84	92	3	0	14	8
8 Acceptance of violence	100	100	83	95	8	5	8	0

9 Black Consc. increasing	100	100	31	20	41	55	28	24
10 Anti-capitalism increasing	100	100	72	70	12	15	16	15
11 Socialism increasing	100	98	61	72	11	15	27	13
12 Radicalism & attitudes to US	93	93	75	71	21	24	4	5
13 View of US corporations	100	100	11	24	72	56	17	20
14 US corporations & liberation	100	100	46	41	43	56	11	3
15 Civil Rights a success in US	86	86	67	72	23	8	10	20
16 US political system	83	90	52	65	31	31	17	4
17 Cubans in Angola	86	86	72	83	11	14	17	3
18 Col. Qaddafi	83	79	47	45	29	33	24	21
19 Israel	76	81	6	3	65	79	29	18
20 US in Nicaragua	57	83	0	6	100	91	0	3
21 USSR in Afghanistan	68	69	8	10	72	75	20	14
22 Polish Govt. & Solidarity	57	71	19	3	48	93	33	3
23 A future foreign policy	95	100						

Non-aligned		Non-aligned Western tend.		Non-aligned Eastern tend.		Pro-West	
58	68	8	2	11	11	17	7

Pro-East		Uncertain	
6	7	0	5

COMMENTS ON TABLE 9

While it is felt that the 93 people - selected in the way they have been - makes for a satisfactory sample, comparison between the two samples of 45 (in 1986) and 48 (in 1987), for purposes of detecting trends or changes, is less satisfactory. Nevertheless, for the purposes of this study it was necessary to make the comparison in order to test if any significant differences were discernible. The observations are therefore very tentative and will be used in combination with a number of other assessments in attempting to draw conclusions about any alteration in attitude over the two years.

1 A few more people may have been ready to see the limitations of US influence in 1987.

2 Either a less critical group, or an indication of slightly less hostility to the US, possibly some of both. Given the rest of the answers it is probably mainly due to the first suggestion.

3 As with 2.

4 More people were clear in the sense of providing answers, which is probably a result of the sanctions debates. Yet fewer people saw a meaningful difference, which is surprising.

5 Very small change, indicating slightly less hostility.

6 As with 5.

7 Given that the 1987 group might be a slightly more conservative one, the fact that a higher percentage saw radicalization as on the increase is noteworthy. It may relate to the impact of the state of emergency.

8 As with 7.

9 Possibly a result of the second group being less sympathetic to the BC movement, possibly a sense that BC's influence had weakened over the year.

10 No change.

11 A small increase in the percentage saying that

socialism was on the increase. Given that the group seemed to be slightly more conservative this may be noteworthy.

12 No change.

13 Second group less negative and more positive about US corporations. Possibly a result of the predisposition of the group, possibly an enhanced appreciation of the positive aspects of US corporations.

14 Surprising given the response to 13. While more people in the second round were more positive about US corporations fewer were positive about the possibility of them playing a positive role in the liberation of Blacks. This may have resulted from the disinvestment experience; people who were favorably disposed now concluding that the companies would not be around to play such a role.

15 Fewer people in the 1987 group were negative about the Civil Rights Movement. Probably as a result of the make-up of the group; as it is unlikely that there has been a reassessment of the movement over the year.

16 Second group slightly more positive about the US political system. Probably more because of the group than a change in assessment. The passing of the sanctions legislation may have caused them to be more positive, but this may also have been counterbalanced by the Iran-Contra scandal.

17 Second group slightly more positive about Cuban presence. Noteworthy, given the predisposition of the group.

18 No change.

19 Increase in the second year is noteworthy. Possibly because of increased hostility. Certainly - to some extent - because of the higher proportion of Moslems interviewed in the second round.

20 Far higher proportion were informed about the issue in the second round. Level of criticism the same.

21 No change.

22 Dramatic increase in the level of criticism of the action of the Polish Government. The only reason that might explain this is that the negative interpretation given by the South African media - originally assumed to be biased - has now been accepted because of an independent source of information on events. This did occur among some trade union people.

23 A small increase in round 2 in support for "pure" non-alignment, mainly at the expense of support for a pro-Western view.

TABLE 10 COMPARING ATTITUDES OF THE TWO GROUPS

Attitude	1986	1987	Total
1 Pro-US	5	7	12
2 Even-handed	3	4	7
3 Moderately anti-US	2	6	8
4 Firmly anti-US	3	0	3
5 Strongly anti-US	12	12	24
6 Extremely anti-US	20	19	39
Total	45	48	93

COMMENTS ON TABLE 10

This table was prepared in the following manner: Each interviewee's answers to every question were assessed in terms of whether they were hostile/negative or friendly/positive toward the US, and then these were added together. Depending on the totals of hostile/negatives and friendly/positives each interviewee was placed in one of the five categories listed in the table.

The main observation to be made is how similar the two group profiles are. Again the very slight differences in the two groups are more likely a reflection of their overall different predispositions than a representation of changing attitudes. If one looks at the first three categories they are more strongly represented in the second year (35% of the total sample) than in the first year (22% of the sample), indicating a moderate reduction in hostility/negativism.

TABLE 11 COMPARING THE ANSWERS TO 10 QUESTIONS OF THE 17 PEOPLE WHO WERE INTERVIEWED IN BOTH ROUNDS

---

1 Personal assessment of US policy of US policy: 1 change from negative to unconditional.

2 Increase in personal sense of anti-Americanism: 5 changes; 4 from yes to no; 1 from no to yes.

3 Distinguish Democrats and Republicans: 5 changes; 2 from no to yes; 1 from no to conditional; 1 from yes to no; and 1 from conditional to no.

4 Blacks anti-American: No changes.

5 Blacks increasingly anti-American: 3 changes; 1 from yes to no; 2 from conditional to yes.

6 Acceptance of violence: No changes.

7 Black Consciousness increasing: 5 changes; 1 from yes to no; 1 from yes to conditional; 1 from conditional to no; 2 from conditional to yes.

8 Anti-capitalism increasing: 6 changes; 3 from yes to no; 2 from yes to conditional; 1 from conditional to yes.

9 Socialism increasing: 8 changes; 1 from yes to no; 3 from yes to conditional; 1 from conditional to

no; 3 from conditional to yes.

10 Future foreign policy: 3 changes; 2 from non-aligned to pro-Western; 1 from non-aligned to "leave it to the people."

COMMENTS ON TABLE 11

In all there were 36 changed responses, and of these 19 amount to "half" changes, for example, from yes to conditional or conditional to no, as opposed to "full" changes, for example from yes to no. Partly this may result from slightly different interpretations of questions; partly from an assessment of some change; and partly from a change in attitude. Many of the changes cancel each other out, and therefore do not indicate any clear trends. In the second round, fewer of the group were as convinced about socialism and anti-capitalism growing, and there was a slight softening of attitude toward the US.

In addition each individual interviewee's answers were compared to test whether anyone had changed his or her overall attitude. Only one person, a manager with a private foundation, who gave 6 different answers, could be said to have done so; and this was from a more radical/anti-American to a more conservative/pro-American attitude.

INDEX

AFRICAN STUDIES

1. Karla Poewe, **The Namibian Herero: A History of their Psychosocial Disintegration and Survival**
2. Sara Joan Talis, **Oral Histories of Three Secondary School Students in Tanzania**
3. Randolph Stakeman, **The Cultural Politics of Religious Change: A Study of the Sanoyea Kpelle in Liberia**
4. Ayyoub-Awaga Bushara Gafour, **"My Father the Spirit-Priest": Religion and Social Organization in the Amaa Tribe (Southwestern Sudan)**
5. Rosalind I.J. Hackett (ed.), **New Religious Movements in Nigeria**
6. Irving Hexham, **Texts on Zulu Religion: Traditional Zulu Ideas About God**
7. Alexandre Kimenyi, **Kinyarwandi and Kirundi Names: A Semiolinguistic Analysis of Bantu Onomastics**
8. G.C. Oosthuizen, S.D. Edwards, W.H. Wessels, I. Hexham (eds.), **Afro-Christian Religion and Healing in Southern Africa**
9. Karla Poewe, **Religion, Kinship, and Economy in Luapula, Zambia**
10. Mario Azevedo (ed.), **Cameroon and Chad in Historical and Contemporary Perspectives**
11. John Eberegbulam Njoku, **Traditionalism vs. Modernism at Death: Allegorical Tales of Africa**
12. David Hirschmann, **Changing Attitudes of Black South Africans Towards the United States**
13. Panos Bardis, **South Africa and the Marxist Movement**
14. Charles O. Chikeka, **Britian, France, and the New African States: A Study of Post-Independence Relationships, 1960-1980**
15. W. Alade Fawole, **Military Interventions in Nigerian Politics**
16. Kenoye K. Eke, **Nigerian Foreign Policy Under the Military Regimes, 1966-1979**